Spiritual Journeys to Other Planets and Past Lives

Case Studies in Quantum Healing and Hypnosis

PAIGE RENEE GARCIA

Praise for *Spiritual Journeys to Other Planets and Past Lives*

"As someone who has remembered and experienced (from as young as age fifteen) my own past lives, I was excited to read *Spiritual Journeys to Other Planets and Past Lives.* Personally I have never used Quantum Healing Hypnosis Technique® (QHHT®) or Reiki Angelic Alchemy Healing® (RAAH®), as I am a Clinical Hypnotherapist and have been trained in Time Line Therapy®; but from reading this book I can plainly see that it is fantastic for anyone who is wishing to find their inner self, who is going through a spiritual journey, or who is just fascinated about where their soul might have gone before living in the Now. As a student of Reiki who believes the body and spirit can be healed with energy, I am interested in the various modalities Paige Garcia has used in the book. I found it thought-provoking reading, where the clients remembered living in past lives, different dimensions, and even living on alien worlds.

"Having re-lived in segments of lives in Egypt, Medieval and 18th Century England, France and more, I believe we are drawn to certain people to learn from in our current life. As both Paige and I have had past lives in Egypt, I wouldn't be surprised if we have met before, as with her and some of her clients in the book. My suggestion when you start reading this book is to free yourself from any limitations of your own beliefs or preconceived notions. There are mysteries and other worlds we have yet to explore, and sometimes due to how we have been raised, our conscious mind can stay closed. Read this book from the viewpoint of that child version of you, the side that loved new things, the one that was intrigued by the supernatural, that questioned the status quo and didn't care what other people thought. Open your mind as you read . . . you might learn something new."

—TANYA FARAMARZIAN

Self-Sabotage Mentor/Master Coach, Intuitive Therapist, Hypnotherapist, Precognitive and Writer

Library of Congress Cataloging-in-Publication Data

Garcia, Paige Renee
Spiritual Journeys to Other Planets and Past Lives:
Case Studies in Quantum Healing and Hypnosis

p. cm.
Paperback ISBN: 978-1-954569-10-2
Ebook ISBN: 978-1-954569-14-0
Library of Congress Control Number: 2025906045
First edition, June 2025

State College, Pennsylvania, USA
(828) 585-7030 · www.CitrinePublishing.com

For information about special discounts for group purchases, please call
(828) 585-7030 or email Info@CitrinePublishing.com.

Contents

Acknowledgments

I would like to thank all those who graciously allowed me to lead them into hypnosis and have given their permission to share the information we retrieved, and have now shared with readers, in this book: Brandi, Jon, Khemistree, Sondra, Brittany, Susan, Wendie, Sandy, and Sara.[1] I would like to thank my editors, Lori Filban and Jaime Cox, for all the hard work they have put into this book. I would especially like to thank my dear friend, Wendie Kingsford, for all the sessions we have had together. I so very much appreciate all the information we have learned from them.

A Note to the Reader

Please read with an open mind, knowing that there is so much we cannot see and do not know. This book is a repository of transcriptions in which clients have discovered their past (and sometimes future) lives, as well as some of the resulting healings, from our quantum healing and hypnosis sessions. These interviews are particularly unique, as some involve discussion around what happened on other planets. The more I learn, the more I realize that there is so much that we do not know.

—Paige Renee Garcia

A Note of Introduction from Beloved Friend, Deborah

Grand Rising, Beautiful Souls,

Within this book, you will find that the unveiling of truths and mysteries will take you on a magical journey as you explore session after session with your determined practitioner and author, Paige Renee Garcia.

Paige and I met through a mutual friend and fellow practitioner, Wendi Kingsford. We were all divinely called to hypnosis modalities known as AURA® Hypnosis and RAAH® Reiki Healing. We each added these modalities to our spiritual arsenal and have moved forward as a soul tribe to battle for the divine healing of humanity.

Paige brings forth an inquisitive uniqueness that leaves no stone unturned when helping to reveal what lies beneath, waiting to be healed and released for the good of her client. In this book, you will experience her unwavering dedication to her mission for humanity and beyond.

As practitioners, we know the unspoken code of honor is service to self through service to others. Paige holds within her a strong and devoted moral compass that shines through all that she does.

As you read through the pages, know that you will be in the highest of divine presence as all of heaven are present and accounted for during these sessions. Put aside all mental boundaries of religion, politics, and what you think you know of our (humanity's) existence.

Free your mind and open your heart. Make way for the power we all hold within and the love of our creator to flow. Accept the beautiful transfer of energy for your own awakening of inner knowledge and greater awareness.

Your author and practitioner, Paige Renee Garcia, invites you to experience the intricate web of soul journeys and the realization that we are in fact the *real* never-ending story.

In Gratitude,
Deborah Jo Cooper
Soul Sister, Fellow Practitioner, Warrior of Humanity

A Note of Introduction
from Beloved Friend, Wendie

In these pages my friend and colleague, Paige Renee Garcia, opens a portal of insight, giving access to the wisdom of the Soul.

As human beings we live in a simulation, a bubble of physical reality in which we choose to have experiences for personal Light expansion. Look beyond this veil that surrounds you, drop the illusions and what is left? *Who are you?* You are in your true form floating in eternity. You are Light. Eternity is not an amount of time but an expansive universe outside of time and space where you exist as pure, conscious loving Light.

It is in this state that I was approached by the being that made himself known to me as Ptah.

As my consciousness expanded into a sea of stars and planets, I became aware of a black hole in the distance. I questioned Ptah as to what would happen if it were to collide with Earth and how this could be averted, as it looked close enough to eventually cause concern. Ptah's response was "Creation is not catastrophe. This is a passage to another dimension." He then showed me the other side of this black hole, a spectacular nebula pouring out streams of conscious Light. As this Living Light takes form, a new dimension begins and this Light begins organizing itself into stars and planets. We are this Living Light and it resides within every cell of our physical bodies.

This matter has been created by us, yet each has its own unique energy imprint and will travel with us on our personal journey of expansion as conscious fractals of our core Light.

We are the Living Light, the Suns, the Stars and the Planets, ever expanding in Love.

May carrying this Consciousness knowing with you illuminate your Divine path and enhance your experience of this book a thousandfold. It is an honor to participate in these pages as one of Paige's clients being gently guided through time and space on a journey of introspection, personal growth, and enlightenment.

Wendie Kingsford
Psychic, Intuitive and Clear Channel

What is the Quantum Healing Hypnosis Technique®?

It is destiny that the early twenty-first century mass popularization of the concept of the *quantum field*—that our physical body and every*thing* in material existence extends electromagnetically beyond itself—would revolutionize the field of hypnotherapy and change the profession forever. Existing as the interstitial space between mind and matter, there are theoretically infinite ways to tap the quantum field for healing purposes. The well-respected regressive hypnotherapist Dolores Cannon led and shaped the ways future hypnotherapists would approach it responsibly and effectively by creating the Quantum Healing Hypnosis Technique® (QHHT®).

QHHT® allows one to tap into ("see") their past and future lives. During a session, clients access their Higher Self (soul consciousness),[2] which offers healing on the soul, body, mind, and/or on emotional levels. The Higher Self can identify physical problems, explain the causes, and direct the body to heal itself. Some of the healings happen immediately, and others happen over time, after the session. The answers to so many questions are within us.

Dolores Cannon developed and refined QHHT® during her forty-five-year career as a regressive hypnosis therapist. She has written many books detailing what she learned in her sessions. She has recovered lost knowledge and has revealed her experiences as an alien and UFO investigator. There are many YouTube videos demonstrating her vast knowledge on these subjects. Her company, which offers accredited courses, remains active today, despite her passing in 2014.

Dolores Cannon taught us that many issues in the body are messages the Higher Self is trying to send to us—there are patterns and meanings for various ailments and discomforts in the body. For instance, if you have a pain in your hips or knees, you may be resistant to moving in a desired direction. Stomach problems often occur because you're holding your emotions in and not releasing them—you are not able to "digest" some words or thoughts.

Through enabling access to past lives, QHHT® allows us to discover the lessons we are each meant to learn, which leads to healing. Sometimes ailments in this life are the result of the traumas from past lives—every life has a purpose and a lesson. Somehow, clients access ("go to") an appropriate past life to find the root of their problems in this current life. For example, one client connected to a past life in ancient times when his whole family was killed—he had to steal food to survive. He could not find employment, as he had no means to get an apprenticeship without family lineage, so he eventually killed himself. When the Higher Self was called into the session, I asked why it chose to show her (the client) that particular lifetime. The Higher Self said that she (he) did not feel worthy in that past life, and thus she did not feel worthy in this life. She was alone in that lifetime, and, in turn, is now alone in this life. She needed to learn to serve herself. She needed to learn dedication to herself.

Another client was married in a past life. His wife left him, and he died alone. When I asked the Higher Self why it brought forth that lifetime, it said that he did not compromise in the past life with his wife and so he died alone—he now needed to learn how to compromise in this life.

A typical QHHT® session is four to five hours. First, the practitioner interviews the client for a couple of hours first to get to know them, to build trust, and ultimately, so that the practitioner knows what kind of questions to ask during the session. The client then lies down, and the practitioner introduces the hypnosis meditation. Next, the practitioner takes the client to the deepest level—where they are able to communicate directly with the greatest source of power and healing there is—what we call the Higher Self. It is the source of all knowledge, and we are an aspect of that Higher Self. We ask the Higher Self to perform a body scan and heal the client. The practitioner can then ask the Higher Self the appropriate questions that the client prewrote, prior to the session, and any clarifying questions that may arise from them.

As you will learn in the next two sections, QHHT® has given rise to other techniques, a blend, which I embrace in my own practice. At the core of my work lies this unique approach pioneered by Dolores Cannon, to whom I remain ever grateful for the ways she cleared out countless pathways for quantum healing on earth and beyond. Please join me in a moment of gratitude.

Other Techniques

Angelic Universal Regression Alchemy Hypnosis® (AURA®) is an expansion of QHHT®. Developed by Rising Phoenix Aurora, AURA® Hypnosis uses a combination of angelic energy work to create a bridge for the client to connect to their Higher Self. Many experience blockages of energy, disabling the ability to reach the deepest possible connection to the Higher Self during hypnosis. So, before the hypnosis, we perform a Reiki Angelic Alchemy Healing (RAAH®) on the client which can remove entity attachments of any sort. We ask to heal blocked chakras and upgrade DNA—there may be inactive strands of DNA that can be activated in a session. We ask to bring back damaged soul fractals (fractals that have split off because of trauma in past lives) so they can be repaired.

We also work with the archangels. We ask Jesus and Archangel Michael to take clients to the healing place which can heal broken fractals of the soul. Aurora also teaches how we can shield ourselves with "I am Source love-light," so that we can manage our energy frequencies in our daily lives, empowering us to be in our sovereignty. We shield ourselves and set our intentions for the day.

She also teaches about archons, reptilians, and gray aliens. Archons come from another universe. They have taken the love light out of themselves and have become artificial intelligence. They have invaded our planet and others. They try to stop us from ascending past the third dimension—our light is food for them. Reptilians can place hooks in us and can be located somewhere else. They work for the archons and suck our energy. Implants are also placed on us to stop us from raising our vibration. Gray aliens come in many forms: some small and some tall. The tall grays were extensively involved in the genetic manipulation of life forms on Earth. They performed hands-on specimen and data collections through physical handling of the human body

There are many techniques born from QHHT® and some of them are used in the sessions to follow. Not only do my clients benefit from these sessions, I myself have also found great benefit from being part of them. It is my great hope and intent that readers will deeply benefit as well.

How Did I Get Here?

I am certified in QHHT® (Level 1 and Level 2), AURA®, and RAAH®. I'm also a certified Reiki practitioner and have training in Regression Healing Hypnosis.

I was raised Christian, but felt I was not getting the truth about God and how we came to be here. So, I read books that expanded my truths outside of the Christian faith. Even as a child, I read many books about past lives, then in the 1980s and 1990s, the metaphysical and New Age books of Edgar Cayce, Ruth Montgomery, and Shirley MacLaine. I found the works of Sylvia Brown in the decades after. I joined the US Military right out of high school in 1982, where I met and married my husband, Mitchell. After three and a half years in the military, I went to work for a company that makes boxes in Northern California.

Within a few years of learning QHHT® and AURA® Hypnosis, I quit that almost lifelong job. Everyone involved with QHHT® has a story of how they heard about Dolores Cannon, and I am no different. In 2018, I was riding my Harley Davidson on the freeway. I was going eighty miles an hour toward Hollister, California, when I heard a voice in my head say, "You're going to get a flat tire." I thought, *No, that's impossible, because these are brand-new tires.* Sure enough, my front tire did go flat. I safely made it to the side of the road, but the bike fell over when I came to a stop. The front tire was partially off the rim—somehow a rock had hit the stem valve, letting the air out. No one I talked with about this incident had ever heard of this happening. I wondered how I was able to survive this with only a scratched knee. I thought, *I must have a purpose in life.*

Shortly afterward, I decided to learn how to meditate. I looked up a YouTube video on meditation. The instructor spoke about Dolores Cannon, so I started watching as many of her videos as I could find. My mind was blown. I had always been fascinated with hypnosis, so in 2019, I decided to take Dolores Cannon's QHHT® course.

Not long after, with one of my clients under hypnosis, I asked what had happened when I got the flat tire on my bike. The client said, "They tried to take you out." I asked, "Who?" The client answered, "The enemy. The ones that don't want the vibrations of this world to rise, like Christ rose. Because in the end, they are the ones that will stand." I asked why it took so long for me to figure out my path. I was told, "Because it was not yet time for you to be activated. Just like many other people in the world can't know yet. Too much chaos and death. Not good, but you are ready." This was not the only time this happened—archangels continued to enter my sessions, telling me they were there to help me.

In September 2019, I went to Mount Shasta, California for in-person Level 2 QHHT® training. Earth has her own chakras, and Mount Shasta is the Root Chakra of the world. It has long been believed by Native American tribes that this dormant volcano has healing powers and a spiritual nature about it—you can feel it when you're close to it. Just like in the human body, there are seven locations around the world believed to be Earth's sacred chakras. They are pockets of energy that are far stronger than anywhere else in the world: Lake Titicaca in Peru is Earth's Sacral Chakra; Ulura in Australia is her Solar Plexus Chakra; Stonehenge in England is the Heart Chakra; The Great Pyramid of Giza in Egypt, the Mount of Olives in Israel, and Mount Sinai in Egypt make up the Throat Chakra; the Third Eye

Chakra has no fixed location (it said to be in Stonehenge right now); Mount Kailash in Tibet is the Crown Chakra.

At the end of the week of Level 2 training, we hiked and meditated on Mount Shasta. That night, as I was putting lotion on my forehead, I felt a strange energy. It was my third eye, starting to open. I now feel this energy in my third eye whenever I meditate, think of certain things, am out in the sun, or do breath work.

Before I left for Mount Shasta in 2019, my Jack Russell, Blondie, would usually cuddle in my arms whenever I lay down, but she had stopped doing this because her back was hurting her. When I returned home from Mount Shasta and the training, I was tired and plopped down on the couch. To my surprise, Blondie jumped up on the couch and nestled in my arms. The energy in my third eye started to vibrate, and we both fell asleep. When we woke, Blondie's back was healed. I asked a friend's Higher Self while under hypnosis, "How did this happen?" She said, "You did that. You received the energy from Mount Shasta. Now practice on your animals, yourself, and other people."

How Wendie
Changed My Life

I always seemed to meet the right people, right when I needed to, often through hypnosis sessions. For example, I put out to the universe that I wanted to learn yoga and I was quickly introduced to a yoga teacher who wanted a QHHT® session. In that yoga teacher's session, her Higher Self told her to learn Reiki and it just so happened that one of my next clients was a Reiki master and teacher. Something told me that I should learn Reiki also, and in December 2019, I met Wendie Kingsford in a Reiki training session. We became good friends, and I asked her if she would like to try a session—her first session with me is in this book.

During the summer of 2020, Wendie informed me that she was going to take the AURA® Hypnosis course. One of the Rising Phoenix Aurora YouTube videos sessions was about how some people's third eye could become encased. So, I asked Wendie if she would go under hypnosis to see if this was the case with my third eye; I was able to see some visions in my dreams, but my third eye was still not fully open. In the session, we found out that my third eye *was* energetically encased. It had become encased while I was in the military—from the vaccine injections. During the session, a beam of light dissolved the case around my third eye, allowing the process of opening to begin. We were told that those who have their third eye encased have to reclaim it.

They have to want it. They have to know it's there—they have to call it back to themselves. We were also told to call upon the angels to guard and protect us in order to transport the third eye back to us safely.

Wendie and I continued to have sessions once a month in which I would facilitate her going under hypnosis. I would then ask questions about the world and sometimes we would do healings on the planet and clear people's energy. Some of our sessions are in this book. In early 2022, we were told to have sessions every Monday, and so we began to do remote healings and energy clearings on other people every week. We were told that the archangels had given us a disc dome sphere in space in order to help heal and energy clear people.

When Wendie and I do a healing and energy clearing together, I make a list of clients' names and what each has asked for. She then goes into a hypnotic state of consciousness after I say her keyword. At this time, Wendie can now actually see their etheric bodies[3] land on an energy sphere from the archangels. When a name is called, it is already set that that person is coming. If they have contacted me, then they have a contract with us and they show up on the sphere with us. For example, I have accidentally called the wrong name (or mispronounced it), and the right person still shows up.

There are times when a person attends as a man, but their human form is a woman. For example, when Wendie communicates with her niece's Higher Self, he is a man, and this person has been a man in most of her past lives. When people needing healing come to our sphere, they choose the form they show up in. We even had one person show up in a race car. (This was a personal sign for him because he had prayed for help during a race event.) We have had people arrive with flowers on their heads, ringing bells, and in different costumes. It all depends on how each person chooses to present themselves when they agree to be called upon the sphere with Wendie and me. There is a frequency and vibration that they ride on.

Whether we call a name wrong or right, we are still reaching out through the frequency, our hearts to them, and they ride that frequency with Wendie, Archangel Michael, and me. This is the process by which one can come out onto the sphere where their Higher Self assists. Healing for one's highest benefit occurs here. We do this by calling in their team of guides; assistance can also come from dragons, mermaids, unicorns, and other entities in the fairy realm and other beings from other realms. Sometimes, we receive assistance from our past life aspects.

Pain in our bodies can be because of entity attachments. One day in exercise class, I noticed pain in my right knee, and I had done nothing to hurt it. When Wendie and I did our session that Monday, we found an entity attachment in the knee. When it was removed, the pain was gone within five minutes. Since Wendie and I have been doing these sessions together, our knowledge and abilities have grown, and Wendie's gifts have grown. She's able to see inside the body and other physical locations, such as someone's property, and scan them. She can see whether you have an entity attachment, implant, or arthritis. She can see why you are having discomfort in any part of your body. Wendie can see if there are any negative entities in your home and clear them. Wendie also has the ability to channel our pets and deceased loved ones.

Sometimes clients have negative portals in their houses in which any type of entity could come through from any dimension. We ask Archangel Michael to close them. Wendie now has a modality which allows her to go up into a client's soul star and speak to the Higher Self, ask questions, and heal past lives. There is also a book of records of every life lived in your soul star, and you can access that in order to heal past lives, allowing healing in this life. Some of our illnesses that come from past lives can be healed.

We each have our own soul star—where our soul resides. We also have stars that contain our whole family. Our soul star is the portal which allows us to access other dimensions, realms, beings, universes, and galaxies—it will allow us to travel wherever we need to go. Our soul star is filled with love and light, and in that place is where we will feel we are home, because this is our soul's home. We only brought one portion of ourselves down into these bodies. Our true home is our soul star. When you look up into the sky, know that one of those stars contains the rest of your soul. Not only do we have homes on other planets and other galaxies, but we have homes in other realms. Our soul star is where we go at night to rest, rejuvenate, and recharge to go over the day's lessons and to plan out the next day.

The Sessions

Brandi

I learned I had a past life with Marie Antoinette, and that I was her best friend in that lifetime. My name was Madame De Polignac. I am also friends in this life with two people who were the royal dressers to the palace and Georgina Duchess, who was good friends with Marie Antoinette and me. One night, I had a vision of my friend Brandi, and I was told that she was also in the life of Marie Antoinette. So, I asked Brandi if she would like to do a hypnosis session with me and she said yes. I thought her Higher Self would take her immediately to that past life (with Marie Antoinette), but I was very surprised when instead, her Higher Self took her to a past life as a spy on another planet. (You never know where you're going to go in a session.) After Brandi went to the past life on another planet, I maneuvered her to the Marie Antoinette life, and I was really surprised by the story that came through. I was so intrigued by Brandi's session that I chose to share it first. Though this was her first session with me, she had had a few with other practitioners.

BRANDI: I see grays or a race that looks similar walking around me. I'm on a street and I'm not on this planet. These beings are not gray though. They are like a green color.

PAIGE: Are they good?

BRANDI: I'm not sure. They're not really noticing me. They are just kind of walking past me. In front of me is just a wall of a building. It almost looks like adobe but it's an odd shape. The corners of the building are jagged. It looks really strange, but nobody's really noticing me. They are just walking past. There's a lot of these beings here.

PAIGE: Does the body feel male or female?

BRANDI: I don't have a sex. When I look down at my body, I am not like these beings.

PAIGE: What do you look like?

BRANDI: I have a form, but I am radiating light. When I look at my hands, my fingers look like suction cups.

PAIGE: How many fingers do you have?

BRANDI: Looks like six or seven on one hand. There's webbing between the fingers. I kind of look like a lizard, but I don't have a solid shape.

PAIGE: Can you see what your feet look like? Are there any toes?

BRANDI: Yeah, I have toes, but it looks like I have two toes, but my body is light. So, it looks like I am glowing.

PAIGE: Are you wearing any clothing?

BRANDI: No. I'm just kind of looking at myself. Looking at my hands. Then when I look up and look around, I'm the only one like myself around here, and I don't think that they can see me.

PAIGE: Do you have any jewelry or ornaments on the body?

BRANDI: There is something on my chest. It's a symbol. There is a triangle with an L shape. It sits in the middle of the triangle and it goes out through the top and the right side.

PAIGE: What does this mean? What does it symbolize?

BRANDI: Seems like this is a device. I think I am cloaked. Yes, this is some sort of device that allows me to be invisible. There's nothing else on this body.

PAIGE: Are you carrying anything with you?

BRANDI: No.

PAIGE: Can you describe what you look like?

BRANDI: I have large eyes. My mouth looks really weird. My head is kind of oval shaped. It's kind of odd. I look very bizarre.

PAIGE: What color is your skin?

BRANDI: The only thing that I can see is bright white light. My whole body looks that way. I have a tail, apparently.

PAIGE: Could you be a reptilian?

BRANDI: That's what it is kind of looking like. I have, like I said, lizard hands and a tail, but I am glowing. I don't know exactly what I am, and I don't know why I am here yet.

PAIGE: Keep moving time and space. Keep moving time. What happens next?

BRANDI: So, I'm inside of this building. There is a big hall. There are a lot of these beings of this alien race on this planet and it looks like some type of assembly. I still do not know why I am here, and I'm listening to what they are talking about. Seems like something about war. These beings are not happy. I think I'm here investigating this race of people, and they are dangerous to my kind. My kind are nonviolent, but these beings are. I'm here to investigate what they are planning. They cannot see me, and they do not know I am here. I'm supposed to report back to the elders of my people.

PAIGE: Why do they want war?

BRANDI: They want resources that they do not have on their planet, and they are going to do whatever it takes to get them.

PAIGE: What kind of resources do they want?

BRANDI: They want a particular type of ore that is on Earth and on other planets. This ore is very important to their people. They use it in a lot of things in their society. What I am understanding is that it is a type of metal, and they will do whatever it takes to get it.

PAIGE: Do you know of any other planets that they have done this to?

BRANDI: There is another planet that they have mined out all of their resources, and this is what is pressuring them now, wanting to find a new resource. They are talking about a neighboring planet to my own. I am here to make sure that they do not succeed.

PAIGE: What do you hear of their plans?

BRANDI: They are arguing about how to move forward—to go about subduing the inhabitants of that planet. They are not willing to negotiate. They are wanting to destroy all the beings on that planet so that they have no resistance. Other parts of this group want to make them slaves so that they do not have to mine the ore and they're arguing about how they need to go about doing it. There are two separate groups, arguing against each other, and this race of people does not speak with their mouths. They speak through their minds, but I'm able to hear them. My race of people also communicates this way. They will not reach a decision today on how to go about this.

PAIGE: Keep moving time and space. Keep moving the scene along. What happens next of importance?

BRANDI: So, they've got ships now. These ships are very large. They have some ships inside of some of the larger ships. The larger ships are just a carrier for the faster smaller ships. They are preparing to invade. They have decided that they will take slaves to mine the ore. Most of the inhabitants will be killed, and it's time for me to go. I have enough information to stop them now. My race of people will defend my neighbor. We are not warlike, but we have ways of stopping war without lifting a finger. We will be helping our neighbor to succeed against these beings. They will not be successful, and I fear that they will turn to Earth next.

PAIGE: What happens next of importance?

BRANDI: I band back with my people. There is a very large building. Everything here looks very strange. The buildings are not familiar. They are all oddly shaped. The sky does not have a sun or a moon, but it has a glow to it that illuminates everything. I am here to relay the information that I have learned to the elders of my people. Now that I am among my people, I realize that I have changed form. My body looks more human now. I have white hair. My skin is very white as well. I'm wearing a white coat and pants made of material that I am not familiar with.

PAIGE: How did you look reptilian when you were invisible?

BRANDI: I can shift to the shape of other beings, as well as cloak, and I do this so if my cloaking device fails, they will not know my true form. That way if I am captured or seen, they will not know what I am, and I can escape. Now that I am back with my people, I am male.

Tall. My skin is smooth. I am here to deliver my report to the leader of my people, and he is not happy.

PAIGE: Who is he?

BRANDI: He is a being like myself and he is much older. He is hundreds and hundreds of years old. He has been our leader for a long time and there are gold cuffs on the sleeves of his garment. Instead of pants, it is sort of like a dress. It's a flowing robe and he wears a headdress that is made out of cloth, and it has a gold disc, just above his head, and he has a staff and wears sandals. He has declared that our neighbors will be protected. We have technology on our planet that allows us to protect our immediate neighbors. We never leave our planet to protect others. We can use our technology. It is a frequency device that we can use to counteract the frequency of another living being. When we broadcast that frequency, all those that do not flee will be destroyed. We can broadcast this frequency *at* the beings that we are after. So, no other beings will be harmed, and he has declared that we will make ready our devices. From the information that we have gathered, we are able to set the frequency of these beings so that they can be destroyed. They will not be successful in harming our neighbor. He has sat back down now and is telling me that I can leave. That I have done my duty. I'm walking back out now and there are people all around me. Well, beings, all around me. We all kind of look the same. Even the women have the white hair and the white skin. Everybody has long hair here.

PAIGE: Keep moving the scene along. What happens next of importance?

BRANDI: There's people kind of running around. Not out of fear, but out of urgency. It looks as though the weapons are ready and it is time to admit the frequency. Suddenly, I can see a large ship on the horizon, and there is kind of a nebula forming beneath it. It's a spinning bluish black portal happening beneath the bottom of the ship. And there is a beam of light coming from the bottom of the ship through this nebula and down to the ground. This is part of the cloaking of this ship. This ship is the weapon. This ship is what powers our weapons on the ground. The beam of light is what powers the ground devices, but the ship will be what we use to admit the frequency this time. We are getting ready. There is a loud booming sound coming from the ship. It is coming in waves. We can hear it throughout our planet, and I can feel it beneath my feet. It's almost as if the entire planet is vibrating. There is a burst of light outside the side of the ship, and we can feel it pass through us. This wave of energy will go out through space in all directions, and this will disrupt the invasion of our neighbor. We will continue to send out waves of this energy and of this frequency and all those that refuse to leave will have their bodies torn to bits. This was a warning. The next pulse will kill anything left that refuses to leave. We are giving them a chance to back off. If they are still there when we send the second pulse, they will be destroyed. I don't know what's happening in space at this time. I just know that the second pulse will come soon. We will give them enough time to flee.

PAIGE: Speed up time and space. Speed up time and space. Did they come back?

BRANDI: We have sent out the second pulse, and our friends on the neighboring planet are protected. Some of the ships remained, and they are now vacant, floating in the space of our neighbor. We have destroyed all beings on those ships. Our neighbors can harvest these ships for their own fleet. These ships will help them understand their enemy, and their enemy's technology, and we will help them as well. These beings will try this again and others of my kind will cloak and go to their planet again and make sure that we are aware of their plans beforehand. We have protected our neighbor.

PAIGE: Were there a lot of people inside those ships that died?

BRANDI: Yes, there were a lot of them that decided not to leave, even though they knew that the frequency was uncomfortable. They thought that was it. They did not know that we were sending them a more powerful pulse that would completely eradicate their life form, but that does not matter. The lives lost are insignificant to the grand scheme of things. Roughly fifty or sixty ships are floating in orbit beside our neighboring planet. They will be able to use these ships for their own good.

PAIGE: Now let's leave that life now. Leaving this person to continue on their own path. They will find peace. Now we are going to go to another place in the past. Another lifetime of importance. Where you were in France. You're drifting and floating. You're going to that lifetime in France. You are there now. What do you feel, see, or know?

BRANDI: There's a woman standing there in front of me with a large, powdered wig. Very elegant gown. Her arms are folded, and her hands are at her waist. She's got white gloves, gold necklace, and her lips are painted bright red, and I am a lady in waiting. I'm part of another influential family.

PAIGE: Do you know who that woman is in front of you?

BRANDI: Marie Antoinette.

PAIGE: What do you feel about her?

BRANDI: I don't like her, but I'm being polite because we are all interconnected in society, and she could have me killed just by speaking it into existence. So, I am mindful of how I speak to her and how I deal with her, but I do not like her.

PAIGE: Why is it that you do not like her?

BRANDI: She cannot be trusted, and she treats people poorly because she knows that she can. She has had many killed because they have spoken against her. I'm very mindful and cunning with the way I deal with her. Sometimes it's best to know that you're dealing with a snake, and she is a snake. We are talking about the political climate of France and how things are going with the monarchy. I'm not terribly interested in the conversation, but I know that I must engage in this conversation and appear to be on her side, even though we are not on her side. My family is not interested in partnering with her in any of her schemes. We will have to appear that way, in order to stay in good grace.

PAIGE: What is one of her schemes?

BRANDI: She is trying to overthrow a Duke and have him removed from power. She has decided to send a young girl there. This young girl, her entire mission is to cause havoc in the duke's life. She has been sent under the guise of helping the Dukes household, but she is an intruder and she will ensure that this Duke has scandal in his family and among his people, and I do not agree with the way she is doing things, but she wants that area for herself and she has some-one that she wants to put in that place where the Duke is. She will ultimately have him assassinated or publicly killed if she has her way, but I am being pleasant, for pleasant sake. I am also gathering information on some of the other things that are going on with the royal family. There's a guardsman and he's coming out and he's asking for her to come inside and she bids me farewell and I'm grateful that I can leave this conversation. So, I'm walking back down the street.

Everyone is dressed very nicely, wearing their best clothing. There are no peasants around. This is a very influential area, and a gentleman is walking up to me now and is asking if I would like to be escorted back home. I tell him that that is fine. He offers me his arm and I'm walking with him back to my home. We're just walking back and he's just talking about regular stuff. The weather and how nice things have been. Complimenting me on my dress. I am not married, and he knows that. I've seen him a few times, but he is not on the list of suitors according to my father, but I don't know enough about him to have an opinion. He seems nice enough but then again, most people seem nice on the surface. So, I am back to my home and there is a doorman here. A guard is opening this really beautiful front door. It's very ornate. It's made out of wood, and he is opening it for me. I'm walking into a courtyard. It's really beautiful. There's a fountain in the middle of the courtyard. I can hear children playing, but I don't see them anywhere. I can hear them laughing and running on the stone, but I don't see them. They must be around the corner, and I'm going back to my father. There's something that I have to tell him. So, my father is sitting in the library, and he is happy to see me. He stands up and puts a hand on each shoulder and kisses me and asks me how my day has been, and I tell him where I've been and he kind of looks at me with a scowl and said, "What is she up to now?" I tell him about her scheme with the duke and he is upset. The duke is a friend of his and he insists that he must send word to him as soon as possible. So, he tells me to leave while he writes a letter to his friend, and he walks over to his writing desk and sits down and pulls out the quill and begins writing. He is very upset about her decision to go after the duke, and he hopes that he is able to stop this before it escalates. So, I walk down the hallway. It's a very long hallway. The right side is open to the weather and has archways. As I'm walking, it's kind of chilly. It's almost like a terrace, overlooking a lot of land

and I am greeted by a servant, and she is asking me, "Are you ready to go to your room?" She will help me undress and I tell her that it is not time yet. That I have not had dinner, and I would like for dinner to be served as soon as possible. She hurries off to the kitchen to let them know to begin serving dinner. I've been out of my home for quite a while today and I am tired.

PAIGE: Let's leave that scene now and go to another important time in this life, where we will find answers that you seek for your highest good. You are there now. Describe what you see or sense.

BRANDI: There is a corral around the gallows and there are two people standing there for the execution. They have been placed in nondescript clothing. It's kind of off-white linen.

PAIGE: Do you know who they are and why they are being killed?

BRANDI: One is the duke. The other is a thief. The duke got involved with the girl that Marie sent and it caused a very big scandal and he is being executed for dereliction of his post. Everybody is having to agree with this because we don't have a choice. If we speak out against this, we will be executed as well, or our material goods will be seized, and we will be left destitute, and without status. We don't have a choice. My father has refused to come today because this is his friend. I am only here because my social status requires it. My father claims sickness to avoid being here, so I am representing our family. My mother died years ago. I am the lady of the house, so I must be here to represent my family. These executions are quite the spectacle. There are vendors and people shouting and people cheering, and it turns into quite a social gathering whenever there's an execution. Whether it's a hanging or a beheading, it doesn't matter. They're slipping the rope around their necks now and I'll look away and pretend that I'm going to a vendor so that I don't see the execution. I have no taste for this type of display. I have spoken to my father and have asked him if we could leave France, and he is considering moving so that we do not have to be near for this. This monarchy has not been good for our country and there has been a lot of turmoil and fear. My father is also looking to remarry, and he does not want to be in France with a new wife. He wishes to move to Greece, and I am happy with that decision. The execution is done, and people are cheering. I'm just finding my way away from the whole thing and I don't want to be here anymore. France is not what it used to be, and it is not what I had hoped to live in and marry in. My father insists that we will find suitors in Greece that are better for our social status than here in France. We have discussed leaving in the spring. I am walking back home now. I have served my social duty. I'm angry. I'm angry that our people and our country have turned into this. That we are fearful to speak up against such travesties. The cowardice that we all live under is distasteful, but it is the only way for us to survive. I will be happy when we make it to Greece. I hear that it is a beautiful place, and we should be able to have social status there, too, that rivals what we have here in France.

PAIGE: Keep moving time and space. Keep moving the scene along, to when something important happens next.

BRANDI: Yes, there is an argument. Marie has confronted myself and my father about us leaving France. She is really angry that we would leave. She had considered us an influential family, she says, and that we are turning our back on France. My father is doing his level best to be civil, but he is losing that battle, and Marie is really angry with us, but my father doesn't want to stay in a country like she has created, and she is angry that my father would say such a thing but, he does not care at this point. We have already sent our belongings forward to Greece. We are set to board the ship this afternoon. My father is more bold because he knows that we are leaving today. Marie is not happy with us and my father just simply doesn't care anymore and I am standing there letting them argue so that I don't get in the middle of it but, there are guards coming up and Marie calls for my father to be seized and I pull a pistol from my sleeve, and I shoot one of the guards. The other guard is completely shocked and taken aback. Marie runs for her life. I do not care what happens to me, but they will not take my father. I fire the last round into the second guard. Marie has run off, screaming. I grab my father and shake him back into reality and we begin to flee the scene. Marie is screaming for the guards and we're running down the street. We know if we can make it to the ship dock, that they will not be able to get to us and we are not far from the ship dock. We are running as fast as we can and we hear the guards coming, but it looks like we are going to make it to the ship dock in time. A shot rings out, but it misses. I can hear the shot echo down the street. Another shot and it misses. They are still too far away for their guns to be of any use. Thankfully, we have made it to the ship dock, and they are allowing us to board. Once we are on the ship, we are outside of the reach of the monarchy. We are in international waters and the guards cannot come after us. We have made it safely on board and the guards stopped their advance. They know that we have gotten away. My father and I are glad that we both have made it on board. We are tired and out of breath from our running, but we are alive and that's all that matters. We will start our new life in Greece and leave this miserable place behind. My father looks at me and says that he is surprised that I had kept my pistol with me and that he was proud of me because I just saved our lives, but he fears that we will not be safe in Greece. That they will send someone to get me because they will consider me a traitor to France because I had murdered two of the royal guards. I am not worried, my father is. "We will cross that bridge when we get to it," I tell him, and I am not concerned because they are unable to come after us directly. They would have to come after us indirectly. We are finding our place on the ship so that we can relax for the evening and we're just walking to our cabin.

PAIGE: Let's leave that scene now and go to another important time in this life where we will find answers that you seek for your highest good.

BRANDI: We have made it to Greece. We have been here for several years now. We have heard word of Marie Antoinette being dead. We are both very happy that she is no longer a threat to us. Over the years she has tried to reach us. Tried to bring us back against charges, but we have always been able to avoid this. My father has a very high status in the government here and we are protected because of that status, but now that she is dead, we do not have to worry about her anymore and we are grateful. I have found a suitor that my father is pleased with, and I am set to be married.

PAIGE: Do you like him?

BRANDI: I do. My father allowed me to choose my suitor. He is a very influential man. Very handsome and very polite. He treats me like a queen and marrying him will elevate my status above my father's and he has ensured that if we are to marry, that I will be able to have anything that I desire. And I have been thinking about what that will look like and I am excited at the prospect. We have been seeing each other for a few months. My father has also taken a bride at this time. He found a very pleasant woman here in Greece. From a very influential family. She was widowed young due to illness and so she and my father have something in common. They are very happy together. She's always chatting. Almost like a little bird just singing away. She hums a lot and sings a lot. She is a good bit younger than my father and has not had children, so they are planning for children. I guess I will be a big sister, after all. My father is very happy and so am I.

PAIGE: Now I would like you to go to the last day in the life that we are looking at and tell me, what is happening?

BRANDI: My husband is kneeled down beside me. He is stroking my hair. I've been sick for quite some time. No one knows exactly what is wrong, but I have been in poor health for quite a while. My hair is gray naturally now.

PAIGE: Did you have any children together?

BRANDI: We had two. A boy and a girl and they are in the front room now. We had a very happy life together and he never disappointed me. He always took care of me and made sure that I had my heart's desires. I have lived a full life, and I am telling him that he has been a good husband and how much I care for him and how much I appreciate the life that we have shared. He is not handling this well and I expected him not to, but I am bedridden now and I am tired of being here. I'm tired of this body. I am tired of being so weak.

PAIGE: Take your last breath in that life and go to the other side. Go to the light.

BRANDI: I just stepped through the doorway.

PAIGE: What do you see on the other side?

BRANDI: It is a white room. Bright, bright white and I'm standing there, looking around kind of wondering what just happened, and an angel is coming. The angel is telling me that it's time to understand everything about my life and to review some things that I needed to learn, and I am going along with him.

PAIGE: What did you need to learn from that lifetime?

BRANDI: I needed to learn courage and how to stand up for what is right. I also needed to learn what a good life looked like. Some of my past lives have not been as pleasant as this one and I am learning that my father is here as well. He had passed many years before myself, and they are saying that after I heal, I will be able to see my father and anyone else that I desire to see. I am in need of rest, integration, and healing and there is time for that now. So, I will begin this process, and the angels will help me with all of this. Part of this experience is me integrating this life into my soul—into my essence, and it may take a while because now I am able to see my life from a higher perspective. From a perspective in union with God, and my life looks different from here than it did living it. So, I will spend some time studying this life to understand all aspects and I can even explore different realities that could have happened in this life based off of decisions that I could have made, and by studying these possibilities, my soul will be able to understand what is needed in future lives and it gives my soul the ability to expand and have a higher awareness of decisions and free will. Ultimately, lives on Earth and other planets teach us about free will. It is one of the greatest gifts that a being can have and I am studying that concept of free will through alternate possibilities of decisions that I made versus decisions that I didn't make, and this will take time. Once this process is complete, I can then decide if I want to go back or if I want to stay here for a while, but I will have future lives from this one. That I know. I am trying to get a higher level of consciousness, and this is the process that one must take to get to that understanding that is required.

PAIGE: Let us leave that life now. You are moving away. Moving away from that woman. Leaving her there so that she may continue on her own path. We are sending her away with love and peace. We now leave that scene with gratitude. Can I please speak to the Higher Self of Brandi?

BRANDI: Yes.

PAIGE: Thank you. I love you; I honor you and I respect you for all of the aid you have given us today. I know that you hold all the records of Brandi's different lives. May I ask questions?

BRANDI: Yes, you may.

PAIGE: Why is it that you chose to show her that life on another planet, where she was watching over the other planet and making sure that they did not harm another planet?

BRANDI: She needs to understand some of these other beings and the lives that they live. I wanted her to see this life to experience life as a different type of being. I have shown her lives leading up to this on other planets and each time they were humanoid. This life was different. Her ability to shape shift is one that is special to that particular type of being, and shape shifting is an essential part of how they go through life. So, at no time do you actually know what they look like, and she needed to experience life as something other than human so that she could understand the complexities of her soul and where she has been and what she has done. Her soul is immense in its knowledge and in this life we showed her what was important in her development at the time she took the role of being a spy for the greater good. She was a key piece in protecting the neighboring planet and it is good for her to see herself in these types of roles. I have shown her lives at the key moments for her development on her journey and this life was important for this stage of her development.

PAIGE: What planet was that?

BRANDI: The name is not something that can be pronounced through the human mouth. It is a sound. A frequency.

PAIGE: Can you tell us the race of the people?

BRANDI: I'm not getting anything.

PAIGE: That is ok. The life with Marie Antoinette—why was my Higher Self telling me that you had a life there?

BRANDI: There was a time when the two of you were linked. There was a time when you each were bonded in that life to understand different concepts of each other's realities. It was a soul contract. You learned from her, and she learned from you. You challenged her and she challenged you. This was all prearranged and agreed upon before incarnation, and being part of each other's soul development is still taking place now. You are both part of each other's journey and in that life, you had special interactions that helped both of your souls advance and that is why it was needed to come to the surface at this time.

PAIGE: Do I have any unresolved karma with Brandi?

BRANDI: No, that has already been taken care of in a previous life. At this point, the two of you are in a mutual agreement to help each other along your spiritual journey and karma is no longer part of the equation. This is solely for the advancement of you both.

PAIGE: Were we friends in the life of Marie Antoinette?

BRANDI: We knew each other but it was more of a social interaction. I would not necessarily call the two of you friends, but you were aware of each other and had social interactions that enabled you both to fulfill your contracts with each other.

PAIGE: What other past lives have I had with Brandi?

BRANDI: There was a time in Atlantis when the two of you were enemies and that has been resolved. Brandi was there at a time when Atlantis was in a state of transition and you were a person that did not see things the way she saw things and the two of you were not friendly towards each other.

PAIGE: I would like to call in Archangel Michael for a body scan. Archangel Michael, could you come in and make sure there's no entity attachments, or implants?

BRANDI: My body feels really heavy.

PAIGE: Archangel Michael, why does her body feel heavy?

MICHAEL: I have paralyzed her temporarily. I am making adjustments to her energy field and while I am here, I would like to deliver a message to Brandi. I have not abandoned you. I have stepped back to allow you to work with your new guides. I know you have wondered where I was, why I haven't had an active role in your development lately, but I am still protecting you. I am making adjustments to her energy field. This is more of an enhancement than it is a correction. It is time for Brandi to advance. This is one reason why this session was needed. It is time for her to advance and this was the best way to get this process started. Brandi does not have implants or spirit attachments, but she does have repeated thoughts. A program that I am removing. We guard Brandi against implants and attachments. At this time, she is at a pivotal part of her development, and it has been decided that it is time for her to move to the next level of understanding.

PAIGE: What is the next level of understanding?

MICHAEL: She will now start to really understand her gifts better as her energy field is being upgraded so that she will have a greater impact on those around her. Her aura will expand and be stronger than it was before. I am adjusting her frequency so that her ability to see into other dimensions will be enhanced. This ramping up of frequency will happen over the next six months. It would be too much for the human body to take all at once. So, we will do it gradually over the next six months. Brandi will start to feel different in her body and this session will allow her to understand why her body feels so strange. She will not be sick, but her body will feel different for a while. Once she reaches the new level of consciousness of frequency her ability to see into other dimensions will shift and she will have a greater impact on the ascension process of Earth. This is necessary at this time. She has passed the test and has proven that she is ready.

PAIGE: Does she have any blocked or misaligned chakras?

BRANDI: Yes. Her Crown Chakra is off balance. It is off-center from the rest of her body, and this has been on purpose. I know she has wondered why things have felt so different with her connection to Source. We have purposely put her Crown Chakra off balance to sepa-rate her from Source to a degree so that she may understand her own power better. It is time to realign this now. Her Crown Chakra will be straight in line now. She now understands how her body works and how her own power will feel different from Source's power. This is key for her advancement. She must be able to distinguish when she is using her own personal power and when she is tapped into the power of the One, and by cutting her off from Source to a degree, she noticed this disconnect and was having to rely on her own abilities and her own skills and frequency, but she has passed the test. She has learned quickly as we had hoped that she would and now we will realign this and she will be fully connected to us again. Now she understands how it feels to be disconnected from Source so that she can now realign herself when she feels that disconnect happen. The rest of her purpose here on Earth is centered around healing others, anchoring light, and helping with the Earth's ascension and she will be most effective when she is connected to Source. Her chakras are now aligned.

PAIGE: Could you also expand her heart?

BRANDI: I can. It is done.

PAIGE: Are there any issues with her auric field[4]?

BRANDI: No, we have helped Brandi keep this part of herself strong. She is able to do this through Reiki and we have taught her through others about auric tears, implants, and kinds of attachments and she has been able to maintain her aura.

PAIGE: Are there any traumas from any past lives that need to be healed?

BRANDI: Yes, but I do not wish to explain those things, I will remove them now.

PAIGE: Does she have any fragmented souls, and will you bring them back to her?

BRANDI: Yes, I am bringing them back now.

PAIGE: How many?

BRANDI: Forty-two.

PAIGE: Can she have a DNA upgrade?

BRANDI: Yes, we will be doing this over the next six months with the frequency upgrade.

PAIGE: Can you scan her body to see if there's anything that needs to be healed?

BRANDI: Yes, I am finding an energetic imbalance in her spine. I am correcting it. It is done.

PAIGE: Thank you. That life that she had in the Egyptian time, was it before Amenhotep?

BRANDI: Yes.

PAIGE: Is there anything that you would like to tell her about that life?

BRANDI: Yes. I know that that lifetime seems very unrealistic. And she has listened to the recording many times, trying to understand the high-level concepts of what we were showing her there. Magic is part of who she is and even though she has forgotten, that lifetime was necessary to do the type of magic that she holds within her. She has had many lifetimes where she has used magic and healing on others. It is important for her to understand the history of where she comes from. Brandi was shown that life for many, many reasons. She has had a lot of questions about Egypt and why she has always felt so connected there, and we felt that it was important for her to finally understand why, and to understand why history never made sense. The human history that people have recorded on Earth of Egypt doesn't even scratch the surface of what actually was Egypt before it was destroyed the first time. Brandi did not die in Egypt—she was taken from that lifetime and transplanted though magic to another place on Earth. Thoth allowed her to escape because it was not time for her life to end at that time. The life that was seen of Brandi, was another life that she had in Egypt. So, she has actually had two lives in

Egypt. This is why she has been so fascinated with the Egyptian people in this lifetime. Yes, her second life violently ended. However, that lifetime was not significant. It did not have the advanced knowledge of her first life, but she had desired to go back to Egypt because she wanted to help bring Egypt back to its former glory. She was unable to do that, and we knew she would be unable to do that, but she was convinced that she could help and she did. That second life was not significant to her soul development at this time. If we deem it necessary to show her that life in another session, we will, but right now at this stage Brandi does not need that lifetime.

PAIGE: The golden ray keeps coming up as part of her journey and she's been told she is a keeper of the golden ray. What does that mean?

BRANDI: Brandi has been a keeper of the golden ray in past lives, and she still is. The golden ray is a very high frequency vibration. This vibration lives within the cells of her physical body, even in this lifetime. She keeps and protects this ray, within her physical body as well as at the soul level. I wish that Brandi could see what her soul looks like. It is a beautiful beacon of golden light. She is truly a keeper of this vibration. This is not a common thing, but Brandi is a very ancient soul and through soul ascension and through various posts that she has had in other lives, she has developed the ability at the soul level to contain this ray and use it. In human form she is not in control of the golden ray. Instead, the golden ray has its own intelligence, and that intelligence works through her and out of her aura and out into space around her. She frequently has strangers look at her directly when they're walking past her. They are not aware of why they are doing this and it is unsettling to Brandi sometimes because the people that are attracted to look at her directly are usually people that are unsavory. They are seeing, at a soul level, the golden ray shining through her eyes and it is helping these people as she passes. She should not be uncomfortable now, knowing this. The golden ray is part of her soul and it is part of who she is. The golden ray is its own intelligence and it is a beautiful frequency of healing. It is very ancient, just like her, and was created for healing on a very deep level. The golden ray is capable of doing many things and can even be harvested as a weapon—if Brandi enters into a situation where her life is in danger, the golden ray would protect her. She would be able to harness this power at that moment enough get out of that situation. Usually, other humans respond to this in awe. They are not aware of what they're seeing, only that what they're seeing they cannot comprehend, and it would give her the ability to escape because they would be dazed and confused at what they just witnessed. Brandi had an experience with the golden ray when she first awakened and she remembers it, but she does not understand what happened at that time. Since she has asked this question, I will explain. Brandi was in the mall and was focusing on the center of her chest, and was saying that she was emitting her light. She was focusing on emitting a light from her body out into public. She wanted people to see the light. She wanted to bring healing to people in public without them knowing, and at that moment, there was a beam of light that she saw coming from her sternum out into public. Out into all the people in the food court. This experience has left her confused over the years as to what happened. That was the golden ray. She had tapped into that frequency and when she emitted it, people in the food court stopped what they were doing and stared at her. She knew at that moment that something had just happened. Something very profound, but until now, we had not had the opportunity to explain to her what had happened. That was the first experience in this lifetime that she had with the golden ray. She was able to utilize it at that moment. Now this happens without her knowing and this is why strangers look at her directly when she is walking past.

PAIGE: Last week she channeled a higher consciousness while she was praying. What being was that?

BRANDI: This was the ALL. What she would say is God. This being, our ALL, our Creator, wanted Brandi to understand what she was, and the message was very clear of his love, and I say "his," only because that is the pronoun she is familiar with, but the ALL does not have a sex. This being is everything. Everything, and Brandi was praying to this being and this being answered her in a way that she was not expecting. He was telling her how much love he has for her and how important her life is in the plan of the universe. He was also explaining that she has forgotten who she is only for a moment in time. That this life only appears separate, but at no point is anyone or anything ever separate from the ALL. There is no possibility of being separate from the ALL, but the human mind will tell you that you are separate because in this existence you are in a physical body that cannot vibrate at the frequency of the ALL, but you are still part of the ALL. It might be a hard concept to grasp for some and Brandi was being reminded that even though she feels like a speck of sand in the universe, that she is still part of the ALL, and the ALL is very proud of who she is and loves her as he loves all of its creation. For the ALL to hate anything in existence with being that the All would hate itself. And that is not possible and the ALL wanted her to understand that she is the daughter of the ALL, and that identity is a very powerful one to remember on this Earth.

PAIGE: In Brandi's last session, it was all about magic. It seemed so deep and fantastical. What was the takeaway information being shared?

BRANDI: We spoke about this earlier. This was important for Brandi to be able to understand what her soul is capable of. Yes, from a human perspective, her previous lives do seem impossible—almost fictional—and she has questioned whether or not what she saw was accurate. It was very accurate. What she experienced is exactly what she was supposed to experience. It was important for her to understand that magic is who she is. Her soul is capable of things that the human mind cannot conceive. She has been on other planets and she was very powerful, and she needed to understand what she actually is. Brandi is a being at the soul level that is very capable of many things. She is an advanced soul, and she needed to understand that in this existence, because her mind is tied to the physical, and it is time to break that connection to the physical. The things that she was shown, her soul is capable of. Being in a human body does not change that and this is a concept that Brandi has yet to grasp. The human body is only a vessel. It is like pouring water into a glass and putting a lid on it. Just because there's water in the glass does not mean that there's not water outside of the glass. The tiny fragment of existence that lives inside of the vessel that Brandi knows as a body, is truly only a tiny fragment of the soul that she is wielding, and this is a concept that is new to her. Seeing herself in these other lifetimes might seem fantastical to the human mind, but this is what her soul is capable of, and the majority of our soul is still in the ethers. Only a tiny fragment is animating the body that she knows to be herself. She still has a full soul. So, being in the ethers, if we were to put numbers to it, 99.999999% of Brandi's soul is still in the ethers. It only takes a small fraction to animate the human suit because that is all this is, a human suit. It gives you the ability to experience a physical reality and to experience free will, but the majority of Brandi's soul is in the ethers and she has full control over her entire soul, as all humans do, and this is a concept that is important because knowing her previous existences and knowing that her majority of her soul is still in ethers, she is capable of anything. The physical reality is only an illusion. We have told her this, but this is a concept that is hard for the human mind to let go of. It is difficult for the human mind to understand that the physical plane is all an illusion. It does not exist. It is a program overlaid and only a small fraction of your true being is actually here and as soon as Brandi can fully integrate this information, she will be able to understand what she is truly capable of. Brandi is a creator being. She can speak into existence things around her—like other humans can—and she is able to harness this, once she understands this concept. She will listen to this recording many times and one day it will click and she will understand what I mean and her life will abruptly change in a way that her mind cannot fathom right now. So, as you listen to this recording, Brandi, know that we are here. Your entire spiritual team you have not met yet. We are here assisting you and protecting you and helping you to remember the very deep and complex fabric of the universe that you are a part of. You are incapable at the moment of understanding this concept fully, but as your frequency and as your spiritual path advances, these concepts will become elementary and you will move on to more deeper truths. This lifetime is filled with very interesting concepts that you will finally remember in human form and when you do, you will be able to bend time in such a way that you will never want for another thing. Dimensions will be able to be skipped across like kids playing in the park. It is a concept that you find very unrealistic, but it is possible in human form because the majority of your being is in the ethers and in the ethers, you are one with the One.

PAIGE: She wants to know how her mother is doing.

BRANDI: Her mother is finished with her soul healing. Her mother is now doing a review of her lifetime. She is exploring mistakes and triumphs and her sickness at this time. She is integrating the life that she just lived.

PAIGE: Is there anything holding Brandi back from having her best life?

BRANDI: The only thing that is holding Brandi back is her ability to let go of the physical. As soon as she is able to let go of the programs that she has told herself, her soul will truly be free of this physical realm, and she will be capable of living her best life. The concepts that I spoke of earlier, she will have to master in order to have her absolute best life, but Brandi is on the trajectory of achieving it. She is advancing faster than we had originally expected her to and we are happy about that. And we are hopeful that she will continue on this trajectory so that she will achieve this higher timeline—her ultimate timeline on this life.

PAIGE: Why does she have such a strong need for sugar?

BRANDI: That is a soothing mechanism. Brandi's childhood was a very dark time for her and at that time, she developed a craving for sugar. It was a self-soothing technique. It is still a self-soothing technique today. She uses sugar to give her body extra energy as well as to create the sensation of calm and she does this in times of high stress, but she also does this when she is happy because it aids her happiness to stay longer. It is a simple habit that she has picked up over the years in order to help herself feel better in her human form. She is able to control this, and she has proved this to herself before, but she does revert back to it in a short order, and that is because this is the one thing that she has found that gives her soothing. She learned at an early age that soothing from another person was not reliable and she has never had any interest in addiction. This is her "addiction," if you want to call it that. This is her self-soothing mechanism. It brings her down from a bad time for encountering low vibrational frequencies. This is an unconscious way of dealing with life as she has found, and now that she understands that it's a self-soothing technique, this will help her understand what is happening when she is so, so hung up on the sugar. It will allow her to be able to walk herself through it and find more stable self-soothing techniques and we will help her with that.

PAIGE: She would like a deeper, more reliable connection to her spiritual team and her spiritual abilities.

BRANDI: That will help with her self-soothing, but she will find physical ways of self-soothing that are more in line with her new frequency. Right now, this is the only one she knows, but now that she is aware of the concept of this being self-soothing, this will allow her to investigate healthier ways in the physical form to self-soothe her physical form and this will help her in a lot of ways.

PAIGE: Is there anything else that her Higher Self would like her to know right now? Anything she needs to correct?

BRANDI: Brandi is on her highest timeline now. She swapped timelines recently, within the last six months. She was aware of it happening. Brandi has gotten to the point where she can see when she skips timelines. This is very helpful because it allows Brandi to know when she has dropped to a lower timeline. In the timeline that she is on now, she is on trajectory to achieving her life mission and goals. There is nothing she needs to change at this time, but she must maintain the course that she is on or else she will fall out of this timeline and experience a lower vibrational timeline, at which time she will have to make further adjustments to get back to this timeline.

PAIGE: The religious spirit is so spiteful, what does her Higher Self have to say about these modern-day Pharisees?

BRANDI: It's bullshit. To use her terminology, religion is nothing. It is a man-made concept of nothingness, and these programmed people are part of the matrix. They are not human in a lot of instances. There is a reason why you cannot reason with this type of human. It is because they do not have the ability to walk outside of the program that their vessel has been programmed with. They are insignificant and unimportant, and even though they are like gnats around your face, do not swat at them, just walk and fly higher than they can. It is unimportant what they have to say about your path. It is unimportant for them to even be in your life. Any type of world religion is futile. It is based on half-truths and mostly lies. It is unimportant and insignificant, and it is a distraction on Earth. Do not be distracted by these beings. They are low vibrational, and they are here to try to knock you off of your higher path. They are incapable of achieving this higher frequency because of the type of being that they are. They are insignificant as long as you allow them to be that way. If you ever engage with them for any length of time or give their program any type of space in your life, it can contaminate the timeline that you are on, and that is their goal. Do not worry about them. Let them pass by and rise above the chatter. They are incapable of harming you in this lifetime. Anything that they do to you, we will automatically correct. It is not an issue, and it is merely part of the matrix. It is merely part of the lower forces on planet Earth that are of slavery to keep as many humans in slavery and bondage and fear as possible, because as the human body fears, it is easier to control, and world religions are all about control. They are a low vibrational experience. A program installed on Mother Earth to enslave and capture and that is its only purpose. These people are not important, and now that you know the truth, it is time for you to explain this to other lightworkers that identify with the Christian label. Tell them what I have just told you and help them rise above as well. World religion is a joke. It is just that. Anything or anyone that comes along to try to knock you off of your path by telling you that you're going in the wrong direction is merely there to hopefully knock you off of your higher path. These beings are from a lower vibration and they're part of slavery on planet Earth.

PAIGE: Is there anything else from her childhood that needs to be released?

BRANDI: Yes. There are still many layers of trauma that Brandi will release over the course of her lifetime. As of right now, there is one layer that must be released at this time in order for her to further advance. This layer is centered around the relationship with her mom and dad. Since her mom has passed, Brandi has been clearing out a lot of information about her mother that was undesirable to Brandi's life, and she has found forgiveness, which is a good starting point. We are currently helping her to dig deeper beneath the surface of that layer and she is working through this in her dream state. She has been shown alternate realities of her mother. These alternate realities have also been collapsed so that her mother can integrate all of these lives at one time. Her mother was in multiple timelines, and we collapsed the majority of them for her mother's higher perspective on every-thing going on in these other timelines. However, there is one aspect of her mother that still lives and still exists in a human form. Brandi has encountered this piece of her mother. This piece is in a higher timeline than any of the other timelines, and this is why her mother has been allowed to keep this existence in that timeline so that she can see what would have happened if she had made better decisions. By understanding this about her mother, Brandi has been able to find forgiveness and understanding of why her mother was the way she was. However, we still have a lot to do with Brandi's father. Brandi has been able to soften her heart towards her father. Only because we have made it so, not because Brandi had intended to. We had to do this, as we explained before, to heal the family bloodline. Because Brandi's bloodline is very important to ascension on Earth. She carries a piece of the original blueprint of the human species. That bloodline is needed when we get to the point of having New Earth. Her bloodline will be part of the blueprint that builds the new human form and she must heal the aspects with her father, and so we softened her heart towards her father to heal that timeline and that bloodline between her and her father's life, because her father's line was the important bloodline. Her mother's was not, but her father's bloodline is abusive and warlike. Brandi has a warrior spirit, but Brandi has a warrior spirit that is different than the warrior spirit of the bloodline she came from, as we explained to her in the previous session. However, there is a part between her father and her that will have to be healed before his passing. She is working towards doing that and we are not at liberty to tell her what that is at this time because if we do, it would alter her ability to heal that naturally and we cannot do that. That would override Brandi's free will and that would violate every law that we have against interference in human lives. She will heal this as she goes along. She and her dad are on the right trajectory to have this happen and when this is healed, a new piece will be healed in Brandi's soul in this life. She is gradually putting things back into position in her life. She is healing faster than we had anticipated in some regards. In some regards, we wish she had healed sooner. This is one of the things that we wish she had been able to heal sooner, which is why we softened her heart, so that she would not miss this opportunity to clear the karma in this life. She was able to clear the karma with her mother before her mother died. We give her the opportunity to speak to her mother and release her mother from karma and release herself from karma. She is on the right path to also do the same with her father. Once that karma is cleared between her and her father, the bloodline will also clear, and that bloodline will be healed. This is significant in many regards, and we are not at liberty to discuss that further.

PAIGE: What was her name in France and her family name?

BRANDI: Pierre was the last name, and Rosetta was her first name.

PAIGE: What has taken me so long to open my third eye more?

BRANDI: There are a lot of things that still need to be healed, and you are on the right path with the work that you are doing. You are learning new things as you go along, and your third eye is actually more open than you think it is. You are blocking your own third eye in some regards. There are things that you are misunderstanding and by misunderstanding, you are clouding your third eye and what your intuition is telling you. My suggestion is to reevaluate some of those things that you have come to understand through your intuition, not through your logical mind. Your logical mind is getting in the way. That's your intuition, because your third eye is already open. It's just that you are not believing what you're understanding, and you are not reaching out with your intuition. You are reaching out with your karmic mind, with your human mind, with your logic. Your logic is not going to be able to get you to the point that you are seeking.

PAIGE: Thank you. Is there anything else that I should have asked that I did not ask?

BRANDI: No, not at this time. Brandi is able to move forward. I am glad that she agreed to have this session with you, and I am glad that you listened to the guidance. We wanted the two of you to have a session soon because Brandi needed to experience new perspectives and we wanted to elaborate more on the session that she had previously, and we also wanted to help you understand the soul connection that you have to Brandi, and why that came up for you and for her. We are happy that the two of you listened to our nudging.

PAIGE: I really enjoyed it. I was amazed and loved the vision you gave me.

BRANDI: We were glad that you listened. It is important to listen in your soul journey, whenever you can, to these nudges.

PAIGE: I fully appreciate it and thank you for all the help that you have given Brandi today. It was just a beautiful, wonderful session. I loved it all.

BRANDI: You are welcome, and we are grateful for you facilitating this information coming through.

THIS SESSION WITH BRANDI WAS held in January of 2023. It is now September of 2024 and I asked Brandi how her life has changed since this session. Here is her reply:

My journey has advanced since our session, in ways that I'm not sure I can really articulate properly. My life doesn't even resemble what it was when we had the session.

The vibrational upgrade was intense and continued even into this year. The QHHT® session that I had earlier this year indicated that I had passed a big milestone and received more upgrades. So, I have been upgrading for awhile now and it has left me feeling very different in my own body and in life. I see things completely differently now. People no longer relate to me in the same ways either. Most of my friends have fallen away.

The golden ray is now fully integrated into my physical being and I can use it in healing others. I also use it to protect myself and my clients. I received the golden ray to use in this way earlier this year. The vibrational upgrades that I've been undergoing have allowed me to consciously utilize this ray in the physical world. It's unreal by the way! It has replaced my Reiki energy, or maybe a better way of saying it is that it is now fully integrated in the Reiki that I channel. My sessions with clients are off the chart now. I've had some amazing confirmations and healings take place in clients this year. I'm more psychic now than I've ever been, and the accuracy has improved considerably as well. I am being taught some new things about my psychic abilities. I'm learning to interpret more detailed messages now.

Religious spirits have been revealed and eliminated from my life. I no longer entertain the conversation. I let them just drone on about this or that and let them die on the vine. I don't have any interest in what they have to say. I see religion as training wheels. If you start with an open mind, you will eventually experience a real spiritual awakening. If you follow along with it, you'll just end up brainwashed. I went from irritating these types of people and being accessible to them, to now, they can't reach me. I've moved past that vibration and now I don't experience this level of ridicule and exposure. Non-soul beings have also come into my awareness, and they are now visible to me. I've met several at work and in public at this point. They are just background people. Soulless and programmed for certain duties, mainly keeping people in line in the matrix system. They are obvious to me now. I even had some on my social media that are no longer connections of mine. I see now though that I am instead inflaming other "light" workers—lots of attacks from false light workers now. That's ok. I'm learning that this too shall pass that I'm being shown the real and the fake.

In the recording, my Higher Self was discussing various topics and kept saying "we." I had assumed that it was my spiritual team and really, I was right, but had a limited view of my team. My Higher Self also said that I had not yet met my whole team. Well, that was true then. Now, I know who and what I am in a deep way. I now work with the council of light, and I am an original member of that council. I come *from the white space. I originated before time and Earth. I was one of the members of the council that seeded Earth originally. I've been on and off planet in many forms. Always coming to Earth to try to help humanity in some way to advance. This is my last incarnation from what I'm understanding. After this life, I will be finished here.*

I also channel the council of light without issue now. I have a direct link to them and their information. It has been like having a QHHT® session whenever I wish to have one. They answer my questions and I have access to high-level information. I am still processing this though because the information seems simple, but it is very far from it.

Dad and I have a working relationship. He and I have seemingly put the past behind us and are now able to have a loving relationship—one that should have been in place the whole time. I'm just grateful that Dad has healed enough, or was humbled enough by mom's passing, that we can now have a relationship. I no longer hold contempt towards him, and I think he is healing in a lot of ways through this new relationship that we have. Part of me is realizing that a lot of the issues originated with my mom and her toxic nature. She was very much a person that enjoyed conflict and I think a lot of the issues with my dad were because of her in one form or another. Certainly not giving the behavior a free pass, but recognizing the greater dynamic between my parents and how they played off each other. Mom is now fully finished with her soul review and healing process. She has now made it to third heaven and is allowed to come to me.

I am now a Karuna Reiki Master Teacher and with that comes a new and elevated vibration which further enhances my abilities and the upgrades that I received both in the session with Paige and in the session earlier this year. I've been in full blown hermit mode since February and am down thirty-seven pounds since then: I can no longer eat the same foods. Sugar isn't even of interest to me on a normal day because it now makes me very tired and run down. My body doesn't react the same way to foods, or maybe I'm more aware of how the foods make me feel afterward. I'm no longer bloated and sluggish. I feel like I've aged in reverse. I really and truly feel like I'm in my twenties again, energy-level wise. I also find that I require more self-care these days. The adjustments that I've received have been intense and have shifted me out of alignment with a large portion of the world. I feel the need for massage, frequent detoxification, and fasting. My self-soothing now is healthier just as my Higher Self said it would be. Food is no longer the "comfort" that it was. Now my comforts are peace and quiet, long ritualized baths, and frequent Reiki sessions with clients.

I also understand myself and my life more. I've been working on harnessing the power that I hold at a soul level. Manifesting isn't as easy as I would hope but I can say that I am seeing big movements in that. I can also skip timelines and I'm aware of doing it. Although I'm not quite as aware of how I did it just yet. Still trying to harness this power because apparently, I'm a bridge between the higher and the lower timelines. I must master this to help others in what is coming. The concept of this body being animated by a small part of my soul is very much an awareness I have now. I know this deeply but I'm trying to navigate how to access my entire soul's power. If I can do this, I know that I can manipulate this experience. I know that deeply, but I have to learn how to do it consistently.

Right now, I'm working on releasing any and all things holding me back. Mindsets, memories, thought forms, energies, beliefs, etc. Releasing daily so I can hopefully grasp more of these higher concepts that I'm being taught.

Jon

Jon was still healing from injuries from a broken back when he came to me. Other than his hearing, he said he did not care about healing his body—he wanted to heal his soul. The extraordinary life he reveals under hypnosis is not only healing of the soul, but of the heart—a journey to which many may relate. Jon wanted just his past life to be told, so that is the only excerpt of the session I have shared below.

PAIGE: What do you see before you?

JON: A cave.

PAIGE: Do you know what's in that cave?

JON: Light, dark.

PAIGE: Have you been in that cave before?

JON: I've seen it before.

PAIGE: What are you doing at this cave today?

JON: Looking.

PAIGE: What are you looking for?

JON: It's a piece of slab.

PAIGE: Piece of slab? For what?

JON: To lay down.

PAIGE: Is that where you sleep?

JON: No.

PAIGE: Why are you in this cave?

JON: Jesus.

PAIGE: Who is the cave for?

JON: Jesus.

PAIGE: What is Jesus going to do in this cave?

JON: He was in it.

PAIGE: What happens next? Could you tell me what happens next?

JON: Nothing.

PAIGE: Why was Jesus in this cave?

JON: It was closed on him. The sun still goes through the cracks.

PAIGE: Can you tell me anything else about being in this cave today?

JON: So dark. Sunlight does come in. *(small pause)* He is behind me.

PAIGE: Who is behind you?

JON: Jesus. He doesn't say anything, but I can feel him there.

PAIGE: Can you tell me more?

JON: It's just a cave. It is where he slept.

PAIGE: Is he talking to you?

JON: No. I can tell he is trying to tell me something. This is where he slept.

PAIGE: What happened to him?

JON: It's where he died. I can see him, but I can't see him. Now he is right behind me.

PAIGE: Hear in your mind what he wants to tell you.

JON: Share his story.

PAIGE: Keep connecting mind to mind and understand what he wants to tell you.

JON: Something about the bed *(slab)*. I see light on it. He is pointing to it. He wants me to lay down.

PAIGE: What happens next?

JON: He is touching my head. He is touching my heart. His face is over me while my eyes are closed. He is giving me a kiss and he says he loves me. He says God is within. I see the sun. It's like I'm flying to the sun.

PAIGE: What happens when you go to the sun?

JON: He is with me, holding my hand.

PAIGE: What else happens?

JON: I'm just flying.

PAIGE: That must be beautiful.

JON: He has long hair.

PAIGE: What color is his hair?

JON: Dark brown. He is smiling. We are flying, or floating.

PAIGE: How does that make you feel?

JON: I feel good.

PAIGE: Where does he take you?

JON: I fly by the sun. I fly around it. He is laughing.

PAIGE: Anything else happening?

JON: I see his halo. He is an angel with wings. He is telling me, "Peace be with you." I'm talking to him and asking him, "Please help me. Protect me. Protect my friends." I'm praying to him.

PAIGE: What happens next?

JON: I'm coming down. I'm going back to the cave. He takes my hand, and we fly up slowly. He has one finger in the air. He is praying for me.

PAIGE: What happens next?

JON: We are flying back to the sun. It is getting really bright.

PAIGE: Can you feel the energy?

JON: I can feel it from my feet to my arms like a tingling feeling. It's really strong.

PAIGE: Is there anything else you notice?

JON: The sky, the stars. Like we are over the sun now. I think he is showing me the universe. We are above the sun. We are above Earth. We are floating above one spot looking around the whole universe. He is laughing.

PAIGE: Why is he laughing?

JON: Joy. He says don't doubt him. He says to share his word. I ask him to heal my heart. He says I have everything. I can heal myself.

PAIGE: Is he healing your ears?

JON: Yes, he is. He has his hands over my ears.

PAIGE: Are you in a past life with Jesus or present life?

JON: It looks like a present life.

PAIGE: Does Jesus have any advice for you?

JON: Believe and preach his word.

Khemistree

Khemistree came to me wanting to know about removing and healing trauma in a karmic relationship. Khemistree has a traditional Christian background but has always felt more love and acceptance when looking into aspects of spirituality versus religion. She had a lot of mixed feelings centered around religious guilt and about being "bad" for looking into spirituality. Although she was conflicted about all the rules and contradictions embedded in her religious upbringing, she needed more answers. I usually ask for the help of the archangels, but Khemistree did not want to work with them because she feared they were part of her false awakening. She loves Jesus, so I asked Jesus to come into the session and help us. Khemistree remembered little of the session.

KHEMISTREE: All the sensations left my body. I can feel myself connecting more with my soul and serving it. I'm looking in on the human me; it's like all the itchiness wanting to run away. Get out of the human body. Don't want to be on Earth. Forgot why she came but knows there's so much more. All how hard that is to remember the impression of what's possible, having to be living in this small box here.

PAIGE: What do you see, sense, or feel about where you're at?

KHEMISTREE: I feel safety in pine trees. It looks like my Higher Self is here and my human-body self and the pyramid is across from me;

behind the pyramid are all these pine trees and they're just on the ground. I feel safe and rooted.

PAIGE: The human body, does it feel male or female?

KHEMISTREE: I'm female.

PAIGE: Can you tell me what the body is wearing? What kind of clothing?

KHEMISTREE: Pink dress, some adornments, jewelry, but the human body looks lifeless. Like she knows it's an attempt to resurrect Lemurian Divine Feminine energy[2], yet the whole matrix system has tried to murder that. So, she looks so beautiful but she's lifeless.

PAIGE: Has she gone back to the time of Lemuria[3]?

KHEMISTREE: Yes.

PAIGE: Can you describe the jewelry she has around her?

KHEMISTREE: Gold, soldered gemstones, and lots of half-circles, like dots.

PAIGE: Is there a purpose for these gemstones?

KHEMISTREE: Protection, healing, contains messages, amplifies beauty.

PAIGE: Tell me why she is in this location. What is happening of importance?

KHEMISTREE: She's trying to move through her somber sorrow of being killed so many times within her Divine Feminine. She's so exhausted trying, trying, trying so many lifetimes and still feeling defeated. She just wants to rest here forever.

PAIGE: Is there anything else you could tell me about this time and place?

KHEMISTREE: The sun is coming over her to resurrect her. She doesn't need to do anything besides sit and bask in the light.

PAIGE: Is her body dying or is she just going out of her body?

KHEMISTREE: She's just going out of her body, and it feels like she's dying—like, that soul pain.

PAIGE: Describe how she takes this soul pain out of her.

KHEMISTREE: She just tries to pretend it's not there. She doesn't know what to do with it.

PAIGE: Keep moving time and space, keep moving the scene along, what happens next?

KHEMISTREE: The sun seems to dump so much life force energy onto her and it looks like a sped- up movie. It just starts to resurrect her, and she dances all around. She got her life energy back, and she knows death is not a real thing, but she believed it for a long time. But now she's dancing and knows that she can't ever die, she can't ever fail.

PAIGE: What happens next?

KHEMISTREE: There's all these people coming, like, in the light shift, and they're the soul family guiding me, but yet she feels mad at them— like they left her and yet she's so happy to see them. Like, longing for them forever. So, it's bittersweet—she wants to run and hug them, but she's not because she felt so alone.

PAIGE: What happens next?

KHEMISTREE: They're coming out of the light shift, and they have this peaceful presence that starts to diminish those angry human feelings, and the front one puts their hand out by the body's heart to help sooth all those feelings.

PAIGE: What do they look like? The people that come out of the light shift? What do they look like?

KHEMISTREE: Three of them are Arcturian[5] and four of them are Pleiadian-dominant,[6] and the Arcturians have like, a red aura around them, so it feels very safe and matter-of-fact and loving. The Pleiadians have a like, purple aura around them and that feels gentle and kind and beautiful. And they just kinda look like me—kind of Nordic, but kind of some other traits. They just look like my family.

PAIGE: What happens next?

KHEMISTREE: Human me is just expressing finally how she felt and is crying as that new energy is being introduced into her field. So, she's finally allowed to just express everything she needs to say that she held in as this new energy is coming out, because it's now safe to say it. And as she just keeps crying she just realizes how silly all those thoughts and feelings were—that they weren't even true, really. She finally breaks down enough to hug them, and they all are in a big group. Like, reunited with love, and family, and connection, and trust.

PAIGE: What did they have to say to her?

KHEMISTREE: You can trust us, we never left you, we were always right there. We never disconnected; you were never really alone. Don't push us away anymore. We are here for you.

PAIGE: So, move the scene along, move the scene along. What happens next?

KHEMISTREE: They invited her into the spaceship and they're going on a ride.

PAIGE: Can you tell me what the inside of the spaceship looks like?

KHEMISTREE: There's a lot of silver and a lot of white. It looks very mechanical and clinical, also some pops of color around with some buttons. And there's some crystals—like tall crystals. I guess you can put your hand on.

PAIGE: What do the tall crystals do?

KHEMISTREE: It's like a divine download automation where you can gather information like Google, and you can manifest things—like where you're going, or telepathic stuff.

PAIGE: Is this a big ship or a little ship?

KHEMISTREE: Kind of small, like maybe seventeen feet across or so. Just enough for seven people.

PAIGE: What is the color of your hair?

KHEMISTREE: Blond. Dirty blond.

PAIGE: What is the color of your skin?

KHEMISTREE: Orange.

PAIGE: Orange?

KHEMISTREE: Yes, orange.

PAIGE: Oh.

KHEMISTREE: That's weird.

PAIGE: What about the Arcturians? What's the color of their skin?

KHEMISTREE: About blue.

PAIGE: What's the color of the Pleiadians' skin?

KHEMISTREE: Purple.

PAIGE: Do the Arcturians have hair?

KHEMISTREE: Yes, but it seems like the beginning when I first saw them—they were cloaked in humanity form.

PAIGE: Ah. Huh.

KHEMISTREE: And now that we're in the ship and trust them and remember them, they let that hologram go.

PAIGE: Oh, I see. So, what does the color of the Arcturians look like?

KHEMISTREE: I think they might not have hair, actually. Their human form had hair that was just black or brown, but I don't think now they have hair.

PAIGE: The Pleiadians, do they have hair now?

KHEMISTREE: Yeah. They still have hair and it's a blondish color, but kind of frizzy. Like maybe some Lyran[7] being in there or something. Kind of maybe mane-like.

PAIGE: So, where is the destination that the spaceship is going?

KHEMISTREE: Home.

PAIGE: Where is home?

KHEMISTREE: Telgeta.

PAIGE: Is that a planet?

KHEMISTREE: It's in the Pleiades system.

PAIGE: Why are they taking you away from Lemuria?

KHEMISTREE: They want me to remember what home feels like again. To help ease my pain of feeling like I'm separated from them or that I'm being punished by being on Earth. They want to remind me what I'm bringing home here on Earth.

PAIGE: Now I'd like you to move the scene along. Move the scene along until you get to your destination. You are now at your destination. Explain what is happening or what you are seeing.

KHEMISTREE: It's like we landed on Telgeta and there's this humongous palace, and it's made of gold that's more beautiful than any earthly gold. It sparkles and it has all this luminescent color, and it feels like this is where I belong. It feels like I just got home after a long trip, and I just can't wait to go inside. Feels beautiful—like Care Bear Land. Nothing could ever go wrong. Not here.

PAIGE: Okay. Move the scene along, move the scene along until something important is happening. What is happening?

KHEMISTREE: I'm going to my bedroom in that palace and there's these two swords on the wall over a fireplace, and it's like I remember these are mine and I pick them up off the wall. Like I'm gonna bring them back with me. Like it's time now to remember my warrior self. Spiritual warrior self.

PAIGE: Can you describe these swords to me?

KHEMISTREE: They're mostly silver or platinum and then they have gold trim. And one red stone on the handle where the cross meets on both sides. They're exactly identical. And they feel mighty.

PAIGE: Can Khemistree bring them back to her in this lifetime?

KHEMISTREE: Yes.

PAIGE: Beautiful. What happens next of importance?

KHEMISTREE: She takes the swords and puts them in her satchel, and they get ready to go back into the ship and leave again like they came specifically for that, and now they're all ready to go back.

PAIGE: Okay. Keep moving time along. Keep moving time along to when she gets back. What happens next?

KHEMISTREE: Well, they go back through the portal and back. To where they first were all together with the pine trees and that clearing.

PAIGE: What happens next?

KHEMISTREE: The one who put out his hand—he's saying goodbyes. The rest of them are in the ship and he's having a serious conversation with me now. Kind of giving me tough love and reminding me of the fact of who I am and what I'm doing.

PAIGE: So, who are you? What does he say? Who do you feel that you are? And what? Does he tell you who you are?

KHEMISTREE: He tells me that I am a positive warrior who specializes in helping fallen systems to be liberated and free, and that playing small was all a part of the matrix system that I was born into and has nothing to do with who I am on a soul level. And kind of is telling me to cut it out—of pretending I'm still so small, and who I really am.

PAIGE: Okay. Move the scene along, move the scene along. What happens next?

KHEMISTREE: He gave me a little crown and then he took off. Now I'm standing here with my swords and my crown and just—nature. Kind of having this feeling—like I'll be running into a dragon I'm supposed to slay or something, which seems to represent the matrix system.

PAIGE: Explain that. Do you mean you'll be turning into a dragon, or? What do you mean by that?

KHEMISTREE: No. Like overcoming a dragon that...overcoming and turning inside out what seems impossible to do but will be "slaying the dragon" so to speak—like as if it's nothing. It's like I know what I'm doing.

PAIGE: Let's leave that scene now and go to another important time in this life where we will find answers that you seek for your highest good. You are there now. Describe what you see and sense.

KHEMISTREE: It's like all of the Divine Feminine outfit came back and that Sleeping Beauty image, and then the whole scene shifted to being in these caverns of crystalline—like Lemuria-feeling, and there's water and it just feels like peace and grace.

PAIGE: What happens next?

KHEMISTREE: The human me gets up from that laying-down position and starts to go into the water, and it just feels enchanted and magical—like she's basking in it. Almost like a spiritual bath just *(muffled)* of these frequencies feeling safe in the beauty.

PAIGE: Keep moving this scene along, moving this scene along. What happens next of importance?

KHEMISTREE: It feels like she moves towards a dark part of the cavern— like to signify something in past lives that's blocking the warrior and the feminine merging in reality. There's still something in the past life, still hidden in the cavern that needs to be transmuted.[8]

PAIGE: Okay. Go ahead and go into the cavern and transmute what needs to be transmuted. Go ahead and go.

KHEMISTREE: It's like so abstract. Like, just this energy of all of the past lives on her that are like she's just going like this instead of having to pick apart, micromanage all the legs, and dissect them. The gist is still the same of all of them. Like suppressed and can't be yourself, can't be true to yourself. Deemed an undesirable or a nuisance or crazy, or whatever; but all of this is now just transmuting. Knowing that that's all that matters. So, the heaviness feels like it's gone. The emotional attachment feels like it's gone.

PAIGE: What was blocking her?

KHEMISTREE: All the fragments of all the lives in the past that didn't work out. It felt like the end and all the deaths, and all the programs, and traumas were like all these little fragments that all together were chaotic but it's starting to swirl and itemize now.

PAIGE: Can she remember how to do this in this lifetime?

KHEMISTREE: Yeah.

PAIGE: Please help her retain that memory on how to do the same thing in this life. Now, what happens next? Keep moving the scene along, moving the scene along, what happens after?

KHEMISTREE: It seems like there's a dragon in the back where that energy was like a—it's like the heartbeat of it all. All the false fallen systems, and it has this iconic energy to the dragon, but he's very deep back in the cavern—like he can't even get out. It's not gonna win at all. Like I'm-gonna-kill-him-type thing. He tries to be scary, but it's just like a program and in this program, I have to slit his neck open. That's just how you get rid of it.

PAIGE: What did you slice? What did you do?

KHEMISTREE: Like knowing that I have to slice his neck.

PAIGE: Oh. Okay. I didn't hear the word "neck."

KHEMISTREE: Like it seems so gruesome and everything—gory, but it's just like a program. Like a matter of fact. This is what you do.

PAIGE: Okay. Keep moving the scene along. Speed up time, speed up time. What happens next?

KHEMISTREE: I'm back where the pine trees are. Like, "what do I do now?" And as I'm pondering that, I look at the trees behind me and I just feel like I wanna build a house.

PAIGE: Let's leave that scene now and go to another important time in this life where we will find answers that you seek for your highest good. You are there now. Describe what you see or sense.

KHEMISTREE: The next scene I have is like standing on top of a steeple of a church and there's nothing anywhere else—just white and blank, and there's just this church that my toes are standing on the tip of the steeple.

PAIGE: What's the purpose of this?

KHEMISTREE: It seems like I need to jump off that steeple. Like it's the last bits of the religious programing that are false. Like, the—all the negativity about like the wrath of God and all this stuff about sin and just, "blah, blah, blah." These things are so unhelpful. It's just spiritual evolution. Like I need to jump free from all of that, and as I jump off of it, I just—I'm like falling in the light, but that's all there is. It's just light. And I'm falling down. I'm just going and there's no harm. So, I guess it's not so scary.

PAIGE: What happens next?

KHEMISTREE: I've fallen to the ocean. I turn into a mermaid and get to swim with the dolphins. So, it seems that I'm a transformer and no matter what is happening I'll be alright, because I know how to transform or something. The state of wonder is great.

PAIGE: Let's leave that scene and go to another important time in this life where we will find answers that you seek for your highest good. You are there now. Describe what you see or sense.

KHEMISTREE: This is like a huge fire, but it doesn't feel scary or intimidating. It feels like knowing some things need to be burned to the ground. Some things need to be fully let go of and surrendered. Like it's being destroyed but, it's for the good. Like the context of all the programs and the matrix system and trauma and things that are meant to be burned up.

PAIGE: Now let's leave that life. You are moving away, moving away from that woman, leaving her there so that she may continue on her own path. We send her away with love and peace. We now leave that scene with gratitude. May I speak to the Higher Self of Khemistree?

KHEMISTREE: Yes.

PAIGE: Thank you. I love you. I honor you, and I respect you for all the aid you have given us today. I know that you hold all the records of Khemistree's different lives. May I ask questions? Why is it that you chose to show her **that** life?

KHEMISTREE: She needs to know who she is.

PAIGE: What were the purpose and the lessons of that life?

KHEMISTREE: So many things are taken so seriously, but they're not really that serious. They're just to evolve, and grow, and to expand, and witness different perspectives.

PAIGE: What does that life have to do with this life now?

KHEMISTREE: It's all integrated as one, so she has all fragments of herself and her soul and gifts of all lifetimes into the mission now.

PAIGE: Is Khemistree free of the matrix now?

KHEMISTREE: 99.9%.

PAIGE: Thank you. Can you describe what is happening?

KHEMISTREE: We are swirling in this dimension that has no pain. There is no such thing. Like Alice down the rabbit hole, but in the cosmic universe where love is only peace, only harmony.

PAIGE: Mother Mary? Can you tell her about the angels? Archangel Michael?

KHEMISTREE: I feel my ego bend in the back, and I feel a weird sensation by my bladder.

PAIGE: Higher Self, what's in the bladder?

KHEMISTREE: Apprehension to say or believe the wrong thing.

PAIGE: I want you to release that. Release that and let your Higher Self be present.

KHEMISTREE: There are so many things in the lower dimensions that have been hijacked and have gotten muddled up with fragments of non-purity. This is a lot, as you see, in the third dimension and the fourth dimension and the fifth. And those even into the higher planes until we get to the Twelfth Dimension[9] which is true, pure Christ-consciousness with divine perfection and divine order. It is best to be very discerning and careful when calling on anything outside of yourself, which is also why Khemistree was so apprehensive even with her soul or star power. Not sure if she could even trust them. Not sure if she could trust *herself.* Not sure if she could trust God or any people.

PAIGE: Okay. Could you help us in the body scan of her body? Could you scan her body for any entity attachments?

KHEMISTREE: There's a heavy chain around her heart that is trying to squeeze the life out of it. It shows up in her life sometimes—as judgment or apprehension in connection with others.

PAIGE: Who's on the other side of this chain? Is there a being on the other side of this chain?

KHEMISTREE: The Archons.

PAIGE: I thought so. Can you put them in the Archon symbol? Put them in the Archon symbol. Put them in the Archon symbol. All of them. How many are there?

KHEMISTREE: Five.

PAIGE: Are they destroyed now?

KHEMISTREE: They're burned up in that fire.

PAIGE: Okay. Good. Did we remove this chain? Are the chains still there?

KHEMISTREE: The chains have gone in the fire.

PAIGE: Okay. Good. Thank you. Keep scanning her body for any entity attachments or implants, cords, hooks, or negative portals.

KHEMISTREE: It's like there is a power button for instant gratification versus things that are not fulfilling, not serving. These can be put on the child of God's mission, confusing them, and distorting the clarity they have going in.

PAIGE: Can you explain that again?

JESUS: There's a negative portal at the back of the head where a power button would be if humans were robots.

PAIGE: Jesus, can you close that portal?

JESUS: So much of this generation being addicted to social media, the internet and TV—it's straining their life force and causing so much confusion by draining their life force out of that part of their body.

PAIGE: Jesus can you close that portal?

JESUS: It's like taking, like cutting off a tube and taking all of the energy to them and plugging it back into God's source. No connection now to a fallen system or black hole portal.

PAIGE: Are there any hooks or reptilian consciousness? Did we find any negative cords, negative implants, negative technology, or wires?

JESUS: There was definitely something impacting the digestive system that was making it hard to disseminate the human experience and now, removed by the fire, will allow more soul self to come into the body. There was also some distortion and fear over the third eye. Just so many times with fear and that's opened and being so different, but now replacing any fear with excitement of wonder and creativity.

PAIGE: That's beautiful. Are there any hooks or reptilian consciousness?

JESUS: Seems like one hook in the back-left shoulder and also some reptilian aspect in the left side in the back as well which is causing all the doubt and apprehension and trying to stop this being from strengthening and moving forward.

PAIGE: Jesus would you please put them in the symbol. Please put all of them in the symbol. In the left shoulder. May I please speak to the entity in the left shoulder? Come up, up, up, up, up. Greetings, I love you, honor you, and respect you. I thank you for speaking to us today. May I ask questions?

REPTILIAN: Sure.

PAIGE: When did you first attach to her?

REPTILIAN: Birth.

PAIGE: Are you related to any of the other reptilians in the body or attached to the body?

REPTILIAN: No.

PAIGE: Are you on the body or are you somewhere else?

REPTILIAN: In the etheric.

PAIGE: What discomfort have you been causing her?

REPTILIAN: Disconnecting her from her soul and life and love.

PAIGE: Do you have a contract with her?

REPTILIAN: Not with her, but her ancestors.

PAIGE: How do you have a contract with her ancestors?

REPTILIAN: They chose me, so I get her.

PAIGE: I want to remind you that all is of love and light, and I would love to help you spread your light so you may be free and go as you please and obtain your own experiences, instead of being stuck in her body. Would you allow me to help you to do that?

REPTILIAN: I guess so, I thought this was the only way.

PAIGE: No, it's not. It's time for you to evolve and have your own life experiences so you don't have to be sucking other people's life forces. You are of love and light and you are part of God, and I'm gonna help you spread your love light, and there's more to this to have your own experiences. ChoKu Rei.[10] Here, using my hands, I am channeling love light to the entities, so they can spread their love light and move on.

REPTILIAN: Wow. No one told me that.

PAIGE: I know. They try to keep it hidden from you. You were also in the matrix.

REPTILIAN: I would like that.

PAIGE: Okay. I'm sending you love light. Start spreading your own love light within yourself. You have that capability. They've hidden and lied to you also. You have light within you. Spread it, spread it all throughout, every bit, and piece, and part of your body. Go ahead and come up. Let me know when you have spread it to every piece and part of your body and make sure you take every piece and part of yourself out of her. Have you spread it to every piece and part of your body?

REPTILIAN: Almost. I have one long, long tentacle still trying to reach for that soul in the belly. It's starting to come up and back to myself now.

PAIGE: Pull it up.

REPTILIAN: Okay. Now I'm going to start to let go.

PAIGE: Okay. Good, good. Let go of her.

REPTILIAN: I really thought this was the only way.

PAIGE: No. It's not. There's so much more than this, and you are stuck there and I'm here to help you. Do you have a message for her before you go?

REPTILIAN: I didn't mean to cause so much harm to your life, being such a bright, shining little person. I didn't mean to hurt you, I just wanted to survive, and I thought this was the only way. Like I was just a parasite sucking your blood and that's all I could ever be. I hope that you can forgive me.

PAIGE: Archangel Azrael, can you show this reptilian on his way where he needs to go? And I'm gonna follow you and see where you go. Can you make sure that he does not get tricked along the way?

ARCHANGEL AZRAEL: Yes.

PAIGE: Speed up time, speed up time. Where do you go? Where do you go?

REPTILIAN: I'm going back into the light. It feels good and safe, and I can even just be me.

PAIGE: Beautiful, beautiful. Thank you. May the light of the Universe always accompany you. Thank you. Okay. I'd like to go back to Jesus. Jesus? You said on the left side and back? Is there one or two there?

JESUS: All of that went with him.

PAIGE: Oh. They all went with him?

JESUS: Yeah.

PAIGE: Beautiful, beautiful. Jesus, can you check all her chakras and make sure they're open and working well?

JESUS: They're all doing okay right now, but the ones that need to be worked on the most to keep consistency are the Throat and the Sacral. Working with these in the color schemes would be very helpful—and sharing and connecting more.

PAIGE: Jesus, at this time can you help her open these up more?

JESUS: Yes.

PAIGE: Thank you. Does she have any false, negative fractals in her?

JESUS: Yes.

PAIGE: How did those get there?

JESUS: The paradigm is filled with fractioning off oneself.

PAIGE: Is there any other healing that needs to be done to those areas?

JESUS: No. Everything is fusing together.

PAIGE: Okay. Good. Is there a fractal—fragmented soul fractals, that can come back to her?

JESUS: Yes.

PAIGE: How many fractals?

JESUS: Seven.

PAIGE: Okay. Can you please bring those fractals back? (*time passes*) Is that complete now?

JESUS: Yeah.

PAIGE: Okay. Are there any contracts that do not serve her that need to be torn up?

JESUS: Yes. One.

PAIGE: What's that from?

JESUS: A contract with the dark or "Satan."

PAIGE: When did she make that contract?

JESUS: At the beginning of her human awakening. She felt compassion for this energy and accidentally let it in, thinking it just needed some love, but yet that conniving spirit turned on her and ran so much havoc in her life. And while she did need that contract...darkness, the ins and outs, it no longer is serving because she knows all about it now. She doesn't need it anymore.

PAIGE: Okay. Please tear up that contract, tear up that contract. Can we heal the trauma from this life and past life?

JESUS: Yes. Absolutely.

PAIGE: Okay. Can we upgrade her DNA? Does her DNA need to be upgraded?

JESUS: Yes. Absolutely.

PAIGE: Okay. Thank you. Upgrade her DNA and please keep working on it through the days, weeks, months. Does she have any negative inter-dimensional beings attached to her?

JESUS: No.

PAIGE: Why did she have Lyme Disease?

JESUS: So she could learn how to heal it. So that she would be so much at the bottom of the well that she would be able to know with exact precision how to help others climb out of that well.

PAIGE: Does she still have Lyme Disease?

JESUS: No.

PAIGE: Okay. Are her digestive issues healed now?

JESUS: No.

PAIGE: What's the root cause of the digestive illnesses?

JESUS: She keeps trying to be like everyone else within the matrix system, yet she is contracted to have a specific, vibrational dietary intake that she keeps trying to rebel against. So, this digestive issue is in place on purpose, to keep her on the right track of having a clear channel.

PAIGE: So, what kind of food is she supposed to be eating and not eating?

JESUS: All of the whole, organic, raw, nature-made foods that are part of the organic timeline, not the stagnant matrix food that is loaded with chemicals.

PAIGE: Can you name those negative foods?

JESUS: The ones that she enjoys the most are these organic chickpea chips. Other than that, her dietary alignment is pretty good, but it's that last remaining piece of trying to fit it and doubting her unique-ness or her vessel.

PAIGE: Could you heal her digestive issues for her?

JESUS: Yes.

PAIGE: Thank you. She would like to know who her partner is to her.

JESUS: This man is her twin flame. You have been through many life-times together which is why it was so hard to get to this point. There are many old stories and traumas from past lives, yet you guys have done great in alchemizing[11] that. There's still so much more to learn and expand and grow together, and you do not need to be afraid of that soul intimacy anymore. You are here to be partners on a mission as warriors in divine love and we are going to heal your fear and doubt and other emotions and traumas related to men so that they will feel safe now.

PAIGE: Who is Nancy to her?

KHEMISTREE: Can I ask you a quick question?

PAIGE: Yes.

KHEMISTREE: Is it too hard to take a fast pee break?

PAIGE: I forgot to explain. When I count to three, get up, and when you come back, you'll be ten times deeper than you were before. One... two...three...Go ahead and open up your eyes and go to the bathroom.

(TIME PASSES)

PAIGE: On the count of three, you'll be ten times deeper than you were before. One, two, three. Feel the relaxation moving through you. Take a deep breath in—as you breathe out, let it go, let it go. I want you to go deeper into relaxing into the session. I want you to feel the Higher Self. Come closer, closer, and closer. Am I speaking to Higher Self now?

KHEMISTREE: Yes.

PAIGE: Are the digestive issues healed now?

KHEMISTREE: Yes.

PAIGE: Why is she itching all the time?

KHEMISTREE: She's itching to get out of her body. She was itching because she couldn't accept the reality of her environment or the constraints of her human body. That is being resolved now, but that was a part of her choice to break down her false mask and the matrix system.

PAIGE: Higher Self, with Jesus, can you scan her body again to see if there's anything else that needs to be healed or cleared from the body?

JESUS: Her right and left-brain hemispheres are starting to just link up centristically—some neurons that were disconnected are just being connected.

PAIGE: Jesus, would you please help her heal more with that? Please help her heal more by connecting those things in her brain.

JESUS: Yes.

PAIGE: Who is Nancy to her?

KHEMISTREE: In past lives she was a great warrior beside you and that is where the connection still is or was in this lifetime. Yet, it's been hard for Khemistree to let her go because of the past connections they've shared, but in this lifetime, she played her role already in childhood and it's okay and safe to let go now.

PAIGE: Who is Mandy to her?

KHEMISTREE: In a past life, they had a very strong connection as there was a queen or princess born to be a queen. And Khemistree, in that life, was her main servant or helper and they had a very strong connection, and that has been why it's been confusing for Khemistree in this lifetime of "who this person is or has been" and the love that she felt for her because of the past life.

PAIGE: Who is Lakota to her?

KHEMISTREE: Lakota is a great cosmic warrior as well, filled with love and joy, who is still on the other plane right now but will be here on Earth indefinitely in the next ten years or less as her child.

PAIGE: Who is Twilight to her?

KHEMISTREE: Twilight will also be her daughter and is on the other plane right now. There have been lifetimes in the past with both of them, and Twilight's essence is full of grace and compassion and moral kindness. All of these qualities within Khemistree and her partner will be amplified within these two perfect little humans. The greatest joy from all the inner work will be that reward.

PAIGE: Who is Randy to her?

KHEMISTREE: Randy was also an ancestor that came before her to help light up the path of individuality and uniqueness. Laughing at his own disabilities in public so that she would have a role model of how it's okay to be different and to take your differences light-heartedly, so he acted as a guide and great friend to be within the family system of this lifetime.

PAIGE: Jesus and Higher Self, can I have one more body scan on her? One more body scan to see if there's anything that needs to be healed or taken away?

JESUS: There's some kind of constraint butchering the heart and throat . . . sorrow. We would like to completely remove that now and put comfort, healing, and love in its place.

PAIGE: Yes, please do that for her. Is that complete?

JESUS: Yes.

PAIGE: Please keep scanning her body—is there anything else that needs to be healed or taken away? Is it complete?

JESUS: Yes.

PAIGE: Thank you. Is there anything preventing her from trust and love anymore?

KHEMISTREE: No. She's just not used to it, and she needs to internalize moving into those frequencies. Even just natural and normal. Writing about those frequencies, singing about those frequencies.

PAIGE: Can you explain to her how she can protect herself from any outside negativity or entities that mean her harm?

KHEMISTREE: By being stronger in your creativity, stepping into your light without thinking. Using your scalar device to move through your chakras, energy clearing and shielding. Doing this whole energetic spin of just dumping all the things that are on you and purging it up and out back to Source. Doing that multiple times a day would be very helpful to get into the routine, so you're shutting off the layers of yesterday. And keeping your gemstone clean and shiny.

PAIGE: Why did she feel like a prisoner inside her body?

KHEMISTREE: Because she knew that this whole system was a prison, and she felt the collective energy to the max. It's almost as if she believed that she had to take it into herself. Transmute it. And there was a time before she felt that way. It wasn't grandiose enough, her adversity story wasn't spectacular enough—like, "oh big deal"—you felt depressed then you felt happy or at peace. But now this chapter of the journey has given her all of that warrior credit that she wanted so that she would have no doubt in her confidence in helping other people who are drowning. And now she has one heck of a story. And she felt that way. Also, so much of the religious programming from when she was little—that she must have done something to "deserve it." And that truly amplified and prolonged so much of that painful torture with, also the things in place, like, all of the implants and all of those things that were keeping her down there. It was the perfect recipe to stop her in her mission, but her soul knew that she would overcome it all.

PAIGE: What is her purpose and what kind of work is she supposed to be doing?

KHEMISTREE: She's supposed to be and will be purifying the bloodlines by helping others that don't understand. Just to remove all the ascension-blockers off of them in a way that's right, easy and as fun as possible, by adding creativity, joy, and music into the mix so it's not all just serious, but it's balanced in how to show people as a way. Show her how to have a balanced, integrated, beautiful life while also serving and evolving and growing.

PAIGE: Does she have any blocks now?

KHEMISTREE: No, she had a really hard block with the warrior meeting the Divine Feminine aspect in this lifetime, and how to bridge the two, but that is why we took her on that journey with everything in the beginning. Because she is both, and she thought those parts were separate where she had to choose one or one was too rough, and one is too soft, but they are integrated as one union, because *both* are needed.

PAIGE: Jesus, do you have any messages for her?

JESUS: Everything that you are looking for is within that clear, Christ-pure, Christ-consciousness that is in, like what we would call, the Twelfth Dimension, so anything below that has the potential to be distorted, or be half-truths, or some ill intent mixed in with truth, so your discernment is getting more and more fine-tuned, and you do not need to judge yourself or anyone else that does anything that is in opposition to what you have learned and know. You just need to lovingly share and teach and speak from your heart—out of compassion and concern, so that we can illuminate all the distortions and distractions from even seeming to be something of interest. Because the core all of this is getting the fallen matrix system back into the hands of love and light and joy and peace and evolution and humanity—dissolving the separation. And while we need to be aware of pitfalls or the tricks, we just navigate more and more intelligently from our soul's higher perspective, that we may see much further and wider than the usual lens humans can see and feel. Sometimes this will feel like judgment, but when you are centered in your heart and have a love for humanity, it is for the greater good to truly follow your discernment, even if you don't know why at the time. Saying "yes" to less things and "no" to more things is going to chip away that very fine path that is meant exactly for just you and your piece of the puzzle. Not to condemn or shame or be higher-up than anyone—just speak from the heart. Be yourself and speak from the heart and share what you have learned. That's it.

PAIGE: Thank you for that. Love, honor, and respect you. Thank you for being here and helping us with this session. Thank you, Higher Self, for being here and helping us today.

Sondra

S ondra studied and practiced shamanism but was unable to help heal herself, only others. She has a neuromuscular disease that gives her muscle spasms. She needed help with her disease, with quitting smoking, and with past-life problems.

SONDRA: Standing on a cliff. It looks like the Grand Canyon.

PAIGE: What do you think you're doing here?

SONDRA: I'm supposed to go down. I see fire and I'm supposed to pull somebody out. I pull my mother out of the fire.

PAIGE: How did she get trapped there?

SONDRA: For her bad deeds. After death. For what she did in life.

PAIGE: Where do you take her?

SONDRA: I just lift her up and we are on the lavender. She is talking to me and asking for my forgiveness.

PAIGE: What do you say back to her?

SONDRA: I forgive you.

PAIGE: Is this *this* life or a *past* life?

SONDRA: This life. Mother says she's sorry for letting the abuse happen. She's sorry for letting me down.

PAIGE: Can you explain where you took your mother?

SONDRA: Maybe the bottom or first level of Heaven. Now I'm going in the opposite direction into the light—the bright sun. There are shadow figures waiting in the light. They are waiting for my father. My father is there. He hugged me. He said he is sorry for letting me down. He is sorry for not protecting me. He is sorry for the abuse.

PAIGE: What do you say back to him?

SONDRA: "I forgive you." Now I'm going to the beach. I see plants and flowers. I'm approaching crystals, animals. My hawk is there. I hug her and she says she will give me a ride. I climb on her, and we are going up. I'm at the cloud and there is blue all around. Archangel Michael is here. We hug. I'm not alone. Raphael is here. Raphael is telling me to just breathe. He sends a green light into my body.

PAIGE: What is the purpose of that?

SONDRA: Healing. He says I need healing from past lives. He says the car accident made me feel what I felt in my last life in Vietnam where I lost my leg. I'm hugging myself as a soldier.

PAIGE: Did you die in Vietnam?

SONDRA: Yes.

PAIGE: What was the purpose and lesson of the Vietnam life?

SONDRA: To learn how to be a warrior. Now I'm on a horse in the desert. I have a sword and I'm in a war. It's old time and I have armor on.

PAIGE: What happens next?

SONDRA: I'm on a train and it's dark. I'm a prisoner of war. I'm skinny and in dirty clothes. I'm hugging myself. Now I'm floating up. I'm going to the desert. I'm at the pyramids. I'm whipping people with a whip to make them work. I hug myself and I turn to dust.

PAIGE: Did . . . you turn to dust? Now I understand. You had to forgive yourself for that life. Where are you going now?

SONDRA: The desert in the city. I'm a magician. I'm a *bad* magician. I'm casting spells. Candles. Goat heads. I hug myself. I go to dust. I go next to where I am a woman on a horse in the desert. I'm at a camp. I'm leaving with the children. As many as I can get. These children were taken prisoner because of war against religion. Islam and Christianity. I got the kids safe. I'm going to go back and get more. The moms are trying to come but I can't fit them. I have to get the kids first. I'm telling them I will be back. I'm back and I'm getting more. Now the mothers are trying to hang onto my horse, and we are going. Some are hanging on; some are falling off. I don't have time. I have to come back. The enemy is coming.

PAIGE: Who is the enemy?

SONDRA: The enemy has shields with red crosses on them.

SONDRA IS DESCRIBING THE KNIGHTS TEMPLAR who had fallen into barbarism. I had a session done on myself recently, and I knew that I had served the Knights Templar. I asked if that was a good thing or a bad thing. I was told in the session that in the beginning of their service the Knights Templar were good. They were of the Cristo energy and had the Emerald Tablets[12] at their fingertips. Later, they were taken over by negative spiritual forces, but the session revealed that I was with the Knights Templar when they were good.

PAIGE: What will they do to the children when they find them?

SONDRA: Torture them and kill them. They are here! I'm grabbing the children and I'm telling the women to run behind me in the direction and that I will be back. I'm on my knees praying to God to help them.

PAIGE: What happens to the people?

SONDRA: They are being raped and killed. I'm in the sand crying and God says I can't save everyone at once. He says I did well. I have faith. I come back with a bigger army. We are fighting. We defeat them. I go get the children and take them to their moms. We are hugging and praying. I've got to move them from this area. The sun is very hot. I took them to a small town, and it is safe. Now I am floating in the air.

PAIGE: Have you passed over from that life?

SONDRA: Yes. A light being[13] is there. We are at a forest with water. It's peaceful. I'm in heaven. There's forest—water falls, animals—it's beautiful. The light being has instructed me on what's to come. He is telling me not to be afraid. To follow him. He is a gate keeper. We walk through a waterfall, through the gate. It's blue and shiny. I go through the gate and there are beings flying in the air in circles. They are coming around me. They are healing me. They put a protective coat on me. Now I'm walking on the beach. Jesus is here. I'm bowing. Jesus says, "My child, you have done a great job." I am free of karmic debt. We are walking hand in hand. I'm asking questions. I ask if I will have to go back. Jesus says it's my choice. I don't want to go back. I choose not to go back. I ask him why I had to live through so many lifetimes. Jesus says I had to learn how to be a warrior and understand pain and agony. Understand fear, understand love. I ask why I had to be put with my parents when I'm completely different from them. Jesus says that I had to understand pain and hurt to become who I am today, and I had to learn no fear to be who I am today. I had to feel the darkness to be able to appreciate the light. Jesus hugs me and then he leaves.

PAIGE: Do you go anywhere else?

SONDRA: There is a giant on the beach. He has silver boots on. I ask him his name and he said it so loud that it knocked me on my back. The vibration of his voice knocked me down on the ground. Zeus says quit living in my head and start living in my heart. Never fear. He shows me my sword.

PAIGE: What does the sword look like?

SONDRA: It has an engraving in the top with three red stones. He puts the sword in my hands.

PAIGE: Do you need the sword in the physical?

SONDRA: Yes. I am now walking in the desert. Bombs are going off in a building because there is a war.

PAIGE: Which war are you seeing?

SONDRA: I don't know for sure. I have on a white, long dress with a train on it and I'm walking in through the middle. I'm a woman with long, brownish-red hair and I'm hovering above the ground. When I walk it sends out a white light. Okay. People are coming behind me. They are strangers. They are scared. I'm hovering above the ground. The numbers are getting bigger. We are going to a mountain. They are safe. Now I'm levitating upwards. I'm getting hit with the blue light and I'm spinning and I'm turning into bluish-purple light. So fast! And I'm catching fire. I just exploded everywhere. I was transmuted into light.

PAIGE: Did you do that to yourself, or did someone else do it to you?

SONDRA: The light beings. Now I'm seeing little fairies. I'm in the forest walking barefoot. I'm wearing a long white gown with a tie around it. I have the same brownish hair . . . long.

PAIGE: Are you in a physical human body?

SONDRA: Yes. I'm walking barefoot. There is a sick deer. I touch him and he is running. There is a baby lamb. It has an arrow through him. I hold him as I take the arrow out. Now he is happy. My hawk has landed on my arm. He is with me. The hawk is teaching me how to fly. He is telling me don't worry, that he won't let me drop. I'm holding on to one of his feathers and we are in the air. He is telling me to let go. I let go and I'm flying. I have wings.

PAIGE: Describe the wings?

SONDRA: They have white feathers like a dove. Now I'm at the ledge. At the fire pit again. I'm going down to see Frank.

PAIGE: Who is that?

SONDRA: My ex-fiancé. He is begging me to get him out.

PAIGE: Is he from this lifetime?

SONDRA: Yes. I grab his hands to bring him out, but this is a trick because he is actually a demon, and he tries to pull me into the pit of fire. I kicked him in the head. Now I'm leaving. My leg is burnt. I heal my leg with my hands.

PAIGE: Where are you going next?

SONDRA: I am a nurse taking care of soldiers.

PAIGE: What war is this?

SONDRA: World War II. There are bodies everywhere. I can't get to them all. We don't have enough help. They are screaming. There is pain and suffering. I go from one person to the next. There are not enough people. There are not enough medical people. My clothes have blood on them.

PAIGE: Move forward in time to another place in time for your healing.

SONDRA: I am not myself. I am an Egyptian God. I am high up and I have a head of a bird.

PAIGE: What is your name?

SONDRA: Isho One.

PAIGE: Can you describe what you are wearing?

SONDRA: White clothing with a tie around, and I'm shooting energy out of my head.

PAIGE: Are you male or female?

SONDRA: Male.

PAIGE: And why are you shooting energy out of your head?

SONDRA: To help a lady with a crown on.

PAIGE: Are you healing her?

SONDRA: Yes. Someone did magic on her. She can barely walk.

PAIGE: Who is the lady?

SONDRA: A goddess.

PAIGE: What goddess?

SONDRA: Athena.

PAIGE: What happens next?

SONDRA: There is a big fire. There is some kind of festival. It celebrates the Day of the Sun. They are bringing me food.

PAIGE: What kind of food is it?

SONDRA: Fruits. And water in a silver cup. The people are little. I'm bigger than the people.

PAIGE: What is your position there?

SONDRA: Ruler of the land.

PAIGE: Can you tell me anything else about this life?

SONDRA: No.

PAIGE: Can you tell me anything else about the Day of the Sun?

SONDRA: Oh no! Someone's getting in the fire; it's a sacrifice.

PAIGE: Did they volunteer to sacrifice?

SONDRA: Yes. There's nothing I could do.

PAIGE: What happens next?

SONDRA: Everybody cheers.

PAIGE: Why do they cheer?

SONDRA: Because they gave the sacrifice to the gods.

PAIGE: Do you agree with this?

SONDRA: No.

PAIGE: Do you try to tell them that they should not sacrifice to the gods?

SONDRA: Yes.

PAIGE: Why don't the people understand this?

SONDRA: They're saying it's been the tradition. I'm leaving. They're acting really rowdy.

PAIGE: Why do you leave?

SONDRA: Their excitement with the woman being sacrificed. They're not good people.

PAIGE: Do you eventually decide to leave them permanently?

SONDRA: I just did.

PAIGE: Where do you go after you leave them?

SONDRA: I'm walking in the desert by myself. I'm on top of the pyramids.

PAIGE: What happens next?

SONDRA: Some light hit me. I walk into the light.

PAIGE: You walk into the light next?

SONDRA: I don't know if I can trust it.

PAIGE: Speed up time. What happens next?

SONDRA: I'm walking into the light; it sucked me up. I'm on a space-ship. There's a reptilian trying to attack me. I use my beak, and I pluck his eyes out. I'm demanding that he lets me go now. Another one appears. The other one appears to try and stop me. I did the same thing. Okay. They're letting me go.

PAIGE: Where do you go afterwards?

SONDRA: They pushed me hard down the pyramid. I'm injured. My whole body's hurting. Every muscle. All of the pain. I can't get up. I'm stuck at the top.

PAIGE: What happens next?

SONDRA: I need help!

PAIGE: Does anyone come to your rescue?

SONDRA: No.

PAIGE: What happens next?

SONDRA: I just lay there. I'm lying at the point of the pyramid. Okay. I'm crawling down. I'm barely crawling down.

PAIGE: Speed up time. Speed up time. What happens next?

SONDRA: I'm lying on my back and a golden white light is coming from the sky.

PAIGE: What happens next?

SONDRA: I'm feeling better.

PAIGE: So, the golden white light heals you?

SONDRA: Yes. And I explode into little bubbles of golden white light. I was fragmented.

PAIGE: So, you lose your body?

SONDRA: Yes.

PAIGE: Now, whatever has happened has already happened and you are on the other side of it. From that position you can see it from a different perspective. Every life has a lesson and a purpose. As you look back at that life, what did you learn from it?

SONDRA: What they were doing was wrong. That sun worship doesn't exist. And the people are not from this. They are not all humans. They are half human, half animal.

PAIGE: Now, let's leave that life now. You're moving away, moving away from that man. Leaving him there so that he may continue on his own path. We send him away with love and peace. We now leave that scene with gratitude. Can I please speak to the Higher Self of Sondra?

SONDRA: Yes.

PAIGE: Thank you. I love you. I honor you. I respect you for all the aid you have given us today. I know you hold all the records of Sondra's different lives. May I ask questions?

SONDRA: Yes.

PAIGE: Why is it that you chose to show her the life of the bird man?

SONDRA: To understand sorcery and witchcraft.

PAIGE: What does that life have to do with her life now?

SONDRA: She was made to fight darkness.

PAIGE: Can I ask the Higher Self, with the help of Archangel Michael, to do a body scan? Do a body scan. Let me know if you see any entity attachments. Do you see any entity attachments?

SONDRA: Right leg and foot.

PAIGE: What kind of entity is it?

SONDRA: Reptilian.

PAIGE: Is it just one or are there two?

SONDRA: Yes.

PAIGE: There are two?

SONDRA: Two. Yes.

PAIGE: The right leg and foot, I would like you to come up, up, up, up, up. May I speak to either the attachment in the right leg or foot? Archangel Michael, put them in the symbol. Put them in the symbol. Okay. I'm going to do the right leg. Right leg, up, up, up, up, up. May I speak to you in the right leg?

REPTILIAN: Yes.

PAIGE: Greetings. I honor you; I love you and respect you. I thank you for speaking to me today. May I ask questions?

REPTILIAN: Yes.

PAIGE: Are you a reptilian?

REPTILIAN: Yes.

PAIGE: When was it that you connected to her?

REPTILIAN: When she was eleven years old

PAIGE: What was the reason for connecting to her?

REPTILIAN: (inaudible)

PAIGE: What discomfort have you been giving her?

REPTILIAN: Pain all over her body from it.

PAIGE: As Earth and the universe is ascending, parasitic entities like you can no longer attach to people. Therefore, we would love to assist you today in spreading your love light so you may ascend. Would you allow me to help you to ascend today?

REPTILIAN: No.

PAIGE: Well, you know Earth is changing, and that if you do not accept to ascend you will be zapped straight back to Source. Would you rather help me help you ascend back into light, and you will be able to evolve and keep the memories that you had? Or would you rather be zapped back into Source?

REPTILIAN: I . . . am . . . *darkness.*

PAIGE: But you can change to light, and I can help you today—change to light and help you evolve. This is not the end. This is just the beginning. You do not *have* to stay in darkness.

REPTILIAN: I made an agreement with my master.

PAIGE: But you can break that agreement. You can break that contract. You do not have to stay dark. You can evolve and ascend to the light. You have that power!

REPTILIAN: No! He's here.

PAIGE: Where's your master at?

REPTILIAN: He's *here.*

PAIGE: Is he on the body or nearby? Is he a reptilian too . . . OHHH . . . Archangel Michael, put him in the symbol. Archangel Michael, put him in the symbol. Put him in the symbol. Archangel Michael, would you take him away? Take him away. Archangel Michael, take him away. Take him away Archangel Michael, take him away. Is he gone?

SONDRA: Yes. I'm awake now.

PAIGE: Archangel Raphael, please come and heal. Heal the area where that reptilian was. Am I still speaking to the Higher Self?

SONDRA: No, it's me. I'm back.

PAIGE: On the count of five, you're going to connect back to the Higher Self. On the count of five. Five: take a deep breath in. As you breathe out, let it go. Feel the relaxation flowing through you. Four: you're traveling through time and space. Drifting and floating, floating and drifting, drifting and floating, floating and drifting. Three: see the ego move on the left-hand side. Further and farther and farther away, allowing the Higher Self to be connected. Two: now the ego mind has moved away and the Higher Self has connected back. One: the Higher Self is here now and we are connected back. May I please speak to the Higher Self of Sondra?

SONDRA: Yes.

PAIGE: What happened that she felt pain?

SONDRA: The demon opened his mouth, and the vibrations caused all her body muscle spasms.

PAIGE: Is that demon still here?

SONDRA: No.

PAIGE: Okay, let's go to the foot. There was a snake on the foot. Is that correct?

SONDRA: Yes

PAIGE: Archangel Michael, put the snake in the correct symbol. Put the snake in the correct symbol. Is there still consciousness in the snake? Does it have any light?

ARCHANGEL MICHAEL: No.

PAIGE: Okay. Do you need Phoenix Fire to transmute it?

MICHAEL: Yes.

PAIGE: Please help me out with the Phoenix Fire. Phoenix Fire on the foot.

MICHEL: Above the knee.

PAIGE: Okay. Above the knee. Let me know when it's been transmuted, Michael.

MICHAEL: Okay.

PAIGE: Thank you.

MICHAEL: Transmuted.

PAIGE: Archangel Raphael, please come in with your green light and heal and seal the area where that snake was. Archangel Michael, please keep scanning her body for any negative attachments or implants.

RAPHAEL: Implants in the head going down both sides of the neck.

PAIGE: Okay. The one in the head, where exactly is it at in the head?

RAPHAEL: Back of the skull running down both sides.

PAIGE: Does it need the Phoenix Fire?

RAPHAEL: Yes.

PAIGE: Okay. Help me transmute it, Michael. Phoenix Fire. Let me know when it's been transmuted.

MICHAEL: It's gonna take time. She was marked when she was born.

PAIGE: What do you mean by "marked?" Can you explain that a little bit more?

MICHAEL: She had a purpose from the Divine. Darkness stepped in to stop her from the Divine.

PAIGE: Mmm.

MICHAEL: She has him in the middle of her back also. Left and right. Third eye has a covering over it. A sheet.

PAIGE: Has the one on the back of the head been transmuted yet?

MICHAEL: Yes.

PAIGE: Okay. Thank you. Okay. Is it an implant at the middle of the back left and right? Is it two implants?

MICHAEL: Four

PAIGE: Can we Phoenix Fire them all together?

MICHAEL: No, one by one.

PAIGE: Oh. Okay. We are gonna go to the middle and the left. Middle left, Phoenix Fire. Let me know when it's been transmuted. Archangel Raphael, can you heal and seal the one area in the head?

MICHAEL: Left complete.

PAIGE: Thank you. Okay. Now we're gonna go to the right. Phoenix Fire. Archangel Raphael, heal that spot; we just took the other one out. Let me know when it's complete.

MICHAEL: Complete.

PAIGE: Okay. Let me know where the third one's at on the back.

MICHAEL: Right side, below.

PAIGE: Right side below, Phoenix Fire.

MICHAEL: Complete.

PAIGE: Thank you. Where's the fourth one?

MICHAEL: Right, below.

PAIGE: Okay. Phoenix Fire, right below. Right, below. Let me know when it's complete.

MICHAEL: Complete.

PAIGE: Archangel Raphael, please heal and seal all the areas where we took those four implants out. Thank you, Raphael. Okay. What is this covering on her third eye?

MICHAEL: To blind her from the spiritual world.

PAIGE: How do we take that off?

MICHAEL: I'm burning it as we speak.

PAIGE: Thank you, thank you Archangel Michael. Let me know when that's complete.

MICHAEL: Complete.

PAIGE: Archangel Michael, keep scanning her for any negative entities, or implants, cords, hooks, or portals.

MICHAEL: Her Root Chakra has a portal.

PAIGE: Please close that portal on the Root Chakra.

MICHAEL: Is it closed now. Complete.

PAIGE: Okay. Archangel Michael, please keep scanning her for any negative implants, cords, hooks, or portals that need to be closed.

MICHAEL: She's been fed black magic through food in her intestines. It is lodged in her intestines.

PAIGE: It's lodged? How do we get that out? Can you take it out for her, Michael?

MICHAEL: Yes.

PAIGE: Okay. Thank you. Thank you. Raphael, can you please heal and seal that area after Michael takes it out?

RAPHAEL: Complete.

PAIGE: Who fed her that food of black magic?

MICHAEL: She knows the name.

PAIGE: Archangel Michael, please keep scanning her of any negative entities, implants, cords, hooks, or portals.

MICHAEL: Bottom right hook.

PAIGE: Say that one more time.

RAPHAEL: Bottom right hook.

PAIGE: Okay. Follow that hook. Where does it lead to?

MICHAEL: Reproductive system.

PAIGE: What's in the reproductive system? How does a hook get in there?

MICHAEL: From a wire. Goes around her reproductive system, keeping her from conceiving another child.

PAIGE: Oh. Does it need Phoenix Fire to transmute that hook? Phoenix Fire?

MICHAEL: No. I'm doing it now.

PAIGE: Okay. Thank you.

MICHAEL: Completed.

PAIGE: Thank you. Thank you, Archangel Raphael. If there's anything that needs to be healed there with your light, go ahead. Are there any more negative entities, hooks, cords, or portals?

MICHAEL: No.

PAIGE: Archangel Michael, what's in her throat?

MICHAEL: Energy.

PAIGE: Why's the energy stuck there?

MICHAEL: Injury.

PAIGE: Injury from what?

MICHAEL: Surgery.

PAIGE: Can you get that stuck energy out of her throat?

MICHAEL: Yes.

PAIGE: Raphael, please heal and seal that area with your green light, her throat. After he loosens the energy. Is that complete?

MICHAEL: Metal.

PAIGE: Metal where?

MICHAEL: Metal in her legs and her neck is reflecting the light. It's confusing the light.

PAIGE: How can we fix that?

MICHAEL: Working.

PAIGE: So, there was metal put in her throat?

MICHAEL: Yes.

PAIGE: Let me know when that's complete.

MICHAEL: Complete. The white light is hitting the reflection of the armor and confusing the light.

PAIGE: Archangel Michael, can you fix that from happening?

MICHAEL: Gladly.

PAIGE: So, is it healed now?

MICHAEL: It's gonna take time.

PAIGE: Okay. I'll ask a couple questions: Higher Self, can you tell her any more on how she's supposed to find the sword?

MICHAEL: It will appear from the husband.

PAIGE: Oh. So, she doesn't need to worry about searching for it?

MICHAEL: He knows where it is.

PAIGE: He does?

MICHAEL: He's trying to control her strength.

PAIGE: How do we get the husband to get the sword then?

MICHAEL: They just moved. He's getting himself together and ready. He wants a place to put it on the fireplace.

PAIGE: How long will it be until she sees the sword?

MICHAEL: Soon. I don't know time frames.

PAIGE: Okay. That's good. Did the Reiki help her that I did in the beginning?

MICHAEL: Yes.

PAIGE: How did it help her?

MICHAEL: It helped her move the darkness that was on her energy field. Darkness comes to her.

PAIGE: Archangel Michael, are you fixing the reflective light on her armor?

MICHAEL: Not complete yet.

PAIGE: Okay.

MICHAEL: Complete.

PAIGE: Thank you. Thank you. Archangel Michael, can you scan her for any Archons on the body? Scan her for any Archons.

MICHAEL: Every chakra besides the Third Eye.

PAIGE: Put them in the symbol. Put them both in the symbol. We're gonna go to the Root Chakra and give it Phoenix Fire. Root Chakra, Phoenix Fire on the Root Chakra. Let me know when it's been transmuted.

MICHAEL: Complete.

PAIGE: Archangel Raphael, heal the Root Chakra with your green light. Did you say the other one was on the Third Eye?

MICHAEL: Third Eye's complete.

PAIGE: Oh. Okay. That's good. Archangel Michael, can you scan her again for any more Archons? Are there any more Archons?

MICHAEL: Every chakra besides the Root.

PAIGE: Can we get them all at once?

MICHAEL: Yes.

PAIGE: Put them in the symbol. Put them in the symbol. Phoenix Fire on all the chakras.

MICHAEL: Complete.

PAIGE: Wow, that was fast! Thank you. Thank you. Archangel Raphael, please heal and seal with your green light every chakra. One more time, are there any more Archons? Any more Archons on her?

MICHAEL: No.

PAIGE: Okay. Good. Can you check all her chakras for being blocked or misaligned? Check every chakra and make sure they're open.

MICHAEL: Open. Complete.

PAIGE: Is her third eye open?

MICHAEL: Yes.

PAIGE: Okay. Can you expand the heart as much as you can?

MICHAEL: Yes.

PAIGE: Archangel Michael, how's the auric field?

MICHAEL: Green.

PAIGE: Beautiful.

MICHAEL: Everything's okay.

PAIGE: Everything's okay with the auric field?

MICHAEL: Yes.

PAIGE: Does she have any negative cords attached to her? Any negative cords?

MICHAEL: No.

PAIGE: Archangel Michael, can you regress her? Regress her in age.

MICHAEL: Yes.

PAIGE: By how many years?

MICHAEL: Forty.

PAIGE: Thank you. Please continue doing that for her through the days. However long it takes, every night or day, to age regress her. Does she have any other negative technology or wires on her?

MICHAEL: Yes. In her brain.

PAIGE: Who put it there?

MICHAEL: Aliens.

PAIGE: What was the purpose of that?

MICHAEL: To control her for the dark side.

PAIGE: Michael, can you please take any negative technology and wires off her brain?

MICHAEL: Complete.

PAIGE: Okay. Are there any more reptilian consciousnesses on her?

MICHAEL: Yes.

PAIGE: Where?

MICHAEL: In the stomach area.

PAIGE: Do I need to talk to it?

MICHAEL: Yes.

PAIGE: Okay. In the stomach. I'd like you to come up, up, up, up, up. Greetings. I honor you, love you, and respect you. Thank you for speaking to us today. May I ask you questions?

REPTILIAN: Yes.

PAIGE: When was it that you connected to her?

REPTILIAN: At the age of seventeen.

PAIGE: Why did you connect to her?

REPTILIAN: To try to get her to kill herself.

PAIGE: What was going on with her that allowed you to come in?

REPTILIAN: Alcohol.

PAIGE: As Earth and the universe is ascending, parasitic entities like you will no longer be able to attach to people. Therefore, we would love to be able to assist you today so that when the ascension comes forth, you won't be recycled straight back to Source—back to zero— losing the experience you gained through being negatively polarized. Instead, we can assist you today to spread your light, helping you to ascend into positive polarization, retaining all the wisdom gained through being negatively polarized. You would be free to incarnate somewhere else, no longer having to feed off others' lights. You would be your own light. Will you allow me to help you today?

REPTILIAN: I am darkness.

PAIGE: I know you're darkness, but you can change. This isn't the end. You've been tricked. You don't have to stay dark. You can ascend into light, and I can help you here today.

REPTILIAN: My master's coming.

PAIGE: Archangel Michael, put the symbol around. Put the symbol around. Put the symbol around the master. Do not let the master come in. Do not let the master come in. Surround her with love lights. Surround her with love light. I'd like the federation of light to surround her. Surround her. Do not let any interference come in. Would you like to go to the light, or would you like to be transmuted back into Source? That's your choice.

REPTILIAN: Source.

PAIGE: Okay. Archangel Michael, take him off. Take him off. Thank you, Archangel Michael, take him away. Archangel Raphael, please heal the stomach with your beautiful love green light. Archangel Raphael, thank you. Archangel Michael, can you please scan her again for any reptilians on her? Any reptilians on her? Keep scanning.

MICHAEL: No.

PAIGE: She's clear. Thank you. Are there any soul fragments that can come back to her now?

MICHAEL: She already completed that.

PAIGE: Okay. That's good. Are there any contracts that we can break? Any negative contracts that we can break?

MICHAEL: They've been broken.

PAIGE: Okay. Can you heal her body from trauma from this life and any past lives? Heal her from the trauma in this life and past lives. Archangel Michael, are there any entities integrated into her DNA?

MICHAEL: Yes.

PAIGE: How many?

MICHAEL: Six.

PAIGE: Can we put them in the symbol? Put them in the symbol.

MICHAEL: Yes.

PAIGE: Do we need to talk to them? Is it possible to get them to go to the light, or do you just need to just take them away?

MICHAEL: Take them away.

PAIGE: Okay. Archangel Michael, please take them away. Archangel Raphael, please heal and seal all the areas where those reptilians were integrated into her DNA. Does she have any interdimensional beings in her?

MICHAEL: No.

PAIGE: Okay. Are there any false beliefs that you can take away from her?

MICHAEL: Yes.

PAIGE: Okay. Go ahead and take those away.

MICHAEL: Complete.

PAIGE: Thank you. Is the vision healed?

MICHAEL: No.

PAIGE: What is the root cause of her vision being blurry?

MICHAEL: The slow stream of energy. Stuck.

PAIGE: Would you heal that? Archangel Raphael, will you heal that?

RAPHAEL: Yes. Complete.

PAIGE: Thank you. What's the reason for her getting hot?

RAPHAEL: The energy's stuck.

PAIGE: Is it still stuck?

RAPHAEL: Leaving in slow stream.

PAIGE: Archangel Raphael, please heal the energy from being stuck. What's the root cause of having Lupus?

RAPHAEL: The demonic attack.

PAIGE: Does she still have the demonic attack?

RAPHAEL: No.

PAIGE: Can we heal the Lupus?

RAPHAEL: Yes.

PAIGE: Okay. Archangel Raphael, go ahead and heal the Lupus. Archangel Michael, let me know when it's complete. Does she have any other blocks?

MICHAEL: No.

PAIGE: Is the Lupus healed now?

RAPHAEL: Complete.

PAIGE: She said she had neuromuscular disease. What's the root cause of that?

RAPHAEL: The implants. Childhood trauma.

PAIGE: Can you heal that for her?

RAPHAEL: Yes.

PAIGE: Thank you. Archangel Raphael, can you scan her body again for anything that needs to be healed? Anything that needs to be healed.

RAPHAEL: Yes, complete.

PAIGE: Thank you. Is there any advice that you can give her for being a warrior? Is there anything you can tell her?

MICHAEL: Love yourself first.

PAIGE: Is there anything I should have asked that I did not ask?

SONDRA: Her addiction.

PAIGE: Her smoking. I forgot all about that. How can you heal her of her smoking?

SONDRA: Need to remove that childhood trauma.

PAIGE: How can we remove the childhood trauma?

SONDRA: From her mother. The abuse.

PAIGE: Would you please remove the childhood—

SONDRA: She does not remember.

PAIGE: Can you please remove that childhood trauma from her mother?

SONDRA: Yes.

PAIGE: Thank you. And every time she tries to smoke a cigarette it will taste really bad. Really bad.

SONDRA: I healed her inner child.

PAIGE: That's good. Is there anything else I should've asked that I did not ask?

SONDRA: She needs to stop letting outside sources interfere with her.

PAIGE: I did not understand that. Can you explain that a little bit more?

SONDRA: She needs to stop letting outside forces interfere with her path.

PAIGE: How can she do that? Can you explain that a little more to me?

SONDRA: She knows what to do.

PAIGE: She knows what to do?

SONDRA: The husband had fears—he used to do exorcisms. She does not know.

PAIGE: How can she help her husband?

SONDRA: She needs to communicate with him. Ask him questions. He was traumatized. One of the patients died. The demonic spirit took over.

PAIGE: Is there anything else that I forgot to ask or should have asked but I did not?

SONDRA: She needs to let go of her son. He will return. He's in God's hands.

PAIGE: Okay.

SONDRA: She asked God years ago to take care of him and he is being taken care of.

PAIGE: That's beautiful. That's beautiful. Is there anything else I did not ask that I should have?

SONDRA: No.

PAIGE: Okay. Thank you. Any other messages for her?

SONDRA: More self-care.

PAIGE: Thank you, Archangel Michael. Higher Self, did we know each other in a past life?

SONDRA: Yes.

PAIGE: We did?

SONDRA: We worked together.

PAIGE: When did we work together before?

SONDRA: We worked together in Turkey healing the blind and the sick.

PAIGE: Okay. At this time, I'm gonna close the session out. At this time, we close this session, any and all beings of light—positively love. All beings of negativity, evil—you are to go to God. Go to Archangel Michael in the name of Jesus Christ, our Lord. You are to be surrounded by God's golden, royal light. You are to leave this session as of right now. We are closing any and all portals with royal golden yellow light. Every portal in her mind, in her body, in her spirit, in this dimension, and in any dark dimension, is closing as of right now.

Brittany

Brittany is also a QHHT® practitioner in the Northern California area located not too far from me. She had never had a hypnosis session done on herself before and was looking for someone she first felt drawn to. I felt drawn to Brittany and offered to mentor her if she needed help. At the time, I was still working my regular job and doing hypnosis sessions on my days off, so we had to wait until I was able. When I eventually contacted Brittany, she was seven months pregnant. When we did the session, I was very excited to discover she was connected to a spaceship. She told me after the session that she has seen Arcturian beings before in dreams and visions, but she never knew who, what, how, or why. This session gave her answers.

PAIGE: Do you feel male or female?

BRITTANY: I want to say . . . female. I feel young.

PAIGE: Do you get a sense of the clothing you are wearing?

BRITTANY: Almost like potato-sack material. Something very cheaply made. And I don't have shoes.

PAIGE: What color is your skin tone?

BRITTANY: Olive.

PAIGE: Now, look at your head. Are you wearing anything on your head?

BRITTANY: No. I don't think so.

PAIGE: Is your hair long or short?

BRITTANY: Short and curly. Maybe I'm a boy.

PAIGE: Do you feel like a boy?

BRITTANY: Yeah. I feel young. I think maybe I'm a boy.

PAIGE: Okay. Are you wearing any jewelry or ornaments on your body?

BRITTANY: A little bracelet. Yarn. Something on my wrist. Just a little bracelet.

PAIGE: Are you carrying anything with you? Bags? Satchels?

BRITTANY: No. Maybe a cloth. Something in my left hand. Something for carrying something.

PAIGE: Is there anything in it right now?

BRITTANY: Yes.

PAIGE: What are you carrying in it?

BRITTANY: A bowl? And maybe a piece of bread. There's a stick in there—I don't know why.

PAIGE: Tell me what else you can sense about the area. Is it dark? Light?

BRITTANY: Light. There's a stone. A pathway. The ground. The pathway. I'm walking up the pathways that leads . . . you can see the ocean. The water. I can see ships on the water. I see ships on the water.

PAIGE: Do the ships have sails on them?

BRITTANY: Yes. Some have sails. Some are big . . . ships. You have to walk down almost like a cliff to get to the ocean. Stairs, maybe—from the pathway—to walk down to where the ships are.

PAIGE: Do you know where you're going yet?

BRITTANY: I'm by myself. I feel . . . it's something that I do every day. I'm walking towards the ship. I don't know if I'm going to learn something. Help somebody. I'm old enough that I'm supposed to be doing this every day. I guess I'm going down to the ships.

PAIGE: Moving the scene along. Moving the scene to when something of importance is happening.

BRITTANY: Okay. I'm at the ship. Maybe I work on the ships or help work on the ships to make money to help my mother. Maybe my . . . I don't know where my father is. So, I work on the ships. On the ships that have the sails. All the ships have grown men on them. So, I don't know if I'm the only child, but they're teaching me how to do this job.

PAIGE: What kind of job are they teaching you to do?

BRITTANY: To prepare . . . to work on the ships . . . to be gone for a long time. I'm not going away right now, but they're teaching me what the ships need, to be gone for a long time. But I'm just helping and learning how to work the ship. How to stock it, to prepare it for travel. I don't know where they're going. They're going exploring. Trades. Exchanging goods. We have . . . olives. Olives and wine in the ship. Olives and wine and oil. Maybe they're going to trade these things.

PAIGE: Keep moving the scene along. Keep moving the scene along to when something of importance is happening.

BRITTANY: Think I'm in my house with my mother. She's frail. She may be sick. She's not old. But she's ... weak. And I'm a little bit older now. I'm helping. She's very weak and frail. I'm trying to feed her, but she's not eating very much. I'm much taller than her now.

PAIGE: Is there anything else of importance you can tell me?

BRITTANY: I think I have to leave on the ship, and I'm nervous about leaving her by herself because I'll be gone for a long time, and she's very weak. And there's nobody else, just me and her. But I have to go on the ship because we need the money. I ask people around us to keep an eye on her, but I'm still nervous about leaving her by herself for so long. Months. Months.

PAIGE: Let's leave that scene now and go to another important time in this life where we will find answers that you seek for your highest good. You are there now. Describe what you see or sense.

BRITTANY: I'm on the ship. There's ... we're in a storm. Some big waves are crashing into the front of the ship. It's dark outside. And the boat is going up and down very hard. I can't see anything around the ship, because it's just water—it's very dark. I'm holding on to something, so I don't fall. Like a pole. Wood. Beam. So, I don't fall.

PAIGE: Keep moving the scene along. Tell me what happens next.

BRITTANY: People are panicking. Securing items downstairs in the boat. Stuff is moving around because the ship is going chaotic. People are scared. It seems to clear up. The water seems to clear up, and it's daytime now, and we are almost there. We're arriving at a dock. And there are men with hats and coats with golden buttons that meet us. I guess we're gonna trade with them.

PAIGE: What do they have to trade with you?

BRITTANY: Maybe some herbs. Maybe fragrance. They don't seem to really have—maybe we're just giving this to them in good faith. Not a gift.

PAIGE: How do you get paid for what you're giving them?

BRITTANY: This is for future . . . for future favors or just showing good faith and we'll have a friendship. Maybe we gave them wine and oil and olives in big barrels for their queen. She's very pleased with this. Good faith. Future friendship. The men have guns. They just carry them. They're not using them or anything. And I'm looking at the gun. It's black and gold. But I've never seen . . . I want to hold it.

PAIGE: Keep moving the scene along. Tell me when something important happens.

BRITTANY: We're back. My mother is very, very, very sick now. She doesn't look like the same person.

PAIGE: How is her health?

BRITTANY: Not good. She cannot get out of the bed. I try to give her some broth. She's very sick. She has a smile on her face because she feels like I'm a man now and can take care of myself. I feel like she's not going to live much longer. I'm happy that I get to see her again, and the people that have been watching her—our neighbors—a man and a woman, they're there. They're comforting. Because she's not going to live much longer, but I'm grateful they took care of her while I was gone. She's going to die soon. But I'm okay with that.

PAIGE: Now let's leave that scene and go to another important time in that life where you will find answers for your highest good. Describe what you see or sense.

BRITTANY: I can't see anything.

PAIGE: You are able to see, sense, know everything very clearly. It's okay. It will become more clear as we speak.

BRITTANY: My mother's gone. I'm older. Much older now. Not old-old, but I'm a grown man and I have a son, Nicholai, and a wife. I still live in the same house. I still work on the ships. My wife is pregnant, and I'm telling my son about the ships and that he can start working on them. He's getting older. And he's very excited about this. And we're just standing on the top of the stone road on the top of the cliff looking down at the ships. And I'm happy, and I think I'm preparing to go away again. And I'm trying to explain that to my son. But I'm not afraid to leave them. My wife and the neighbors all care for each other.

PAIGE: Now let's leave that scene and go to another important time in this life where we seek answers for your highest good. Describe what you see or sense.

BRITTANY: I'm on the ship. It's nighttime. The water is calm. And looking at the stars. I'm just . . . I'm at peace. I'm just happy. My family is content. I'm content. And I just . . . I'm thankful. I feel at peace—just feel at peace.

PAIGE: Now leave that scene. Let's go to the last day of your life in this life. What do you see?

BRITTANY: I'm an old man. I have gray hair. I'm in my bed. And my wife is sitting, holding my hand. She's sitting on the bed with me. I'm lying down. I have a grandson. My grandson is there. And my son—he's grown now. And they're all looking down, smiling at me. Everybody. I'm just at peace. I know I'm gonna leave soon because I saw my mother the same way. I'm not as sick as her. I just know it's time. And I'm at peace, my family is happy.

PAIGE: Take your last breath and go to the other side. What happens next? Where do you go?

BRITTANY: I'm shot out of the top of my head, backwards. And it's dark, but I can see. I feel like I'm floating. It sparkles. There's a little light. Twinkle lights. Just kind of floating.

PAIGE: Speed up time until you get to your destination. Speed up time. Where do you go?

BRITTANY: I just see colors. Color clouds. I'm just floating. I'm just taking a break. It's dark here, but there's clouds and sparkles, and they're different colors. I'm just floating through them. Relaxing. I don't . . . I can go somewhere if I want to. But I'm choosing to take a break.

PAIGE: Now you are on the other side of it. What has happened has already happened and you are on the other side. From that position, you can see it from a different perspective. Every life has a lesson and purpose. As you look back at that life, what did you learn from it?

BRITTANY: How to be happy and feel content with simple things. Simpler. Just find joy and peace in everything. I didn't have much, but I was very happy. My family was happy. They were healthy. I had a job where I could take care of them. I had my health. I had peace.

PAIGE: Now, let's leave that scene. You are moving away from that man—leaving him there to continue on his own journey. We send him away with love and peace. We now leave that scene with gratitude. Can I please speak to the Higher Self of Brittany? May I please speak to the Higher Self of Brittany?

BRITTANY: Yes.

PAIGE: Thank you. I love you. I honor you and respect you for all the aid you have given us today. I know that you hold the records of all Brittany's past lives. May I ask questions?

BRITTANY: Yes.

PAIGE: Why did you choose to show her that life?

BRITTANY: So that she could know what matters and that state of peace. You don't need a lot of things or to be all the things that society tells you you need to be. What matters is your family, your peace, and your health and your contentment.

PAIGE: What were the purpose and lessons to that life?

BRITTANY: Stability. She felt very stable in that life. She was able to take care of her family. Everybody had exactly what they needed. Nothing more. Nothing less. She was okay with that. Everything was provided. She operated within flow of love and energy. And everything was provided. She didn't have to worry or stress about anything.

PAIGE: What does that life have to do with her life now?

BRITTANY: She wants to have that sense of peace and stability and operate within flow. She tries, but she does let outside things disrupt that and it throws her off. And she worries about stability. Even though everything will be provided if she just stays within the flow. And stops looking at outside things to dictate how her life should be. But she does pretty good, but sometimes she allows herself to get worried or stressed about things.

PAIGE: I'd like the Higher Self to perform a body scan. Would you like help from any of the archangels?

BRITTANY: Yes. Michael, Raphael.

PAIGE: Archangel Michael, please be with us here today. And Archangel Raphael. Archangel Michael, please help with the body scan. Please scan the body for any entities, implants, hooks, or portals.

MICHAEL: There is something in the head. It was put there. Like a little antenna that turns.

PAIGE: Is this a negative implant?

MICHAEL: I don't know. No.

PAIGE: Does it need to be removed?

MICHAEL: Not right now.

PAIGE: What is the intention of this thing in the head?

MICHAEL: Transmute thoughts. Radio frequencies outside of the planet. To some sort of ship. It's connected to a ship. They can stay connected and see what is going on.

PAIGE: What are the names of these beings connected to the ship?

MICHAEL: I want to say Arcturians.

PAIGE: Arcturians.

MICHAEL: They're watching over the planet. Their ship is over the planet. It's a very large ship. She chose to come here for this mission. They're watching. It looks like a ship.

PAIGE: Can we connect to the Arcturians on the ship? Can I speak to someone on the ship?

ARCTURIAN: Yes.

PAIGE: Greetings. I love, honor, and respect you. Thank you for being with us today. Who am I speaking to?

ARCTURIAN: I'm on this ship.

PAIGE: What position on the ship do you hold? Are you the captain? Can you explain that to me?

ARCTURIAN: I do watch over some of the others on the ship, but I'm a watcher. I watch the planets, what's taking place. Events for the timeline to see where we're at. How everything is coming together. Like puzzle pieces. Just monitoring that.

PAIGE: Why did you choose her to have a radio frequency with?

ARCTURIAN: She wanted to be our eyes and ears on the planet. She wanted to. She volunteered. So, we allowed her to go to Earth. To be our eyes and ears in human form. Because we cannot interfere with free will. So, we're able to see life through her eyes. We can see what she feels as a human because we don't have the same capacity, so we're able to see what she feels as three-dimensional. We can understand somewhat logically, but not the feeling of it. That's what we have her for.

PAIGE: Could you tell me why she decided to volunteer for this job?

ARCTURIAN: The experience of it. It gets a bit boring here after a while. And we're here for a very long while. And she wanted to not just watch, she wanted to experience and feel what it's like rather than just being told from a logical sense of what humans experience. She wanted to experience what it was like to be a human, so she would have a better understanding and be able to teach us from that experience and not just from the perspective of how we view humans.

PAIGE: How are we doing as a whole? As humans on the timeline?

ARCTURIAN: There is a very large shift that has taken place. Split consciousness. So, some are going backwards and staying the same, and some are moving at a faster pace to a higher consciousness. But that's their choice. And we're just watching. There's a bigger divide than there was before.

PAIGE: Is there anything we can do as a whole to help people get on the right timeline so we can get on the right path?

ARCTURIAN: Not everybody is going to make it this time around, but they will be able to come back with that knowledge they have learned and move with the higher consciousness of the planet. Some people are just not going to align with the frequency of the planet anymore where it is going and they are going to exit, but they will be able to gain knowledge and come back if they choose to. They don't have to come back, but the planet is raising very fast, so if you don't align, you don't have the capacity to align with the new energy. Then you will choose to exit because it will look like fear to you, and you will be scared. Although that's false. That's not real. That's something you've created in your mind.

PAIGE: Some people here have been duped into getting the vaccine. Will they still be able to ascend?

ARCTURIAN: Some will. Once they realize what it is that they have done. That they have been tricked. Once they see the system for what it really is. The vibration to which they rise up to will dissolve it. What they put in their body won't work anymore. This is a free will thing. Your free will allowed you to be in fear enough to take the vaccine and your free will will allow you to break through. It's your choice if you want to stay in fear or if you want to stay in love frequency. It's your choice. But once you see it for what it really is, step out of fear into love, and it will dissolve.

PAIGE: Do you have any messages or other advice for us?

ARCTURIAN: There are a lot of people waking up at this time. But, there are so many people who are getting sucked down farther and farther into the control and the fear, and we just wish, we just hope for them to be able to see, because everyone on this planet is needed at this time. Everybody has something to contribute, no matter how big or small. The ones that perpetuate the fear don't have as much control, but they still have a strong hold on a lot of people. And those people really need to step into love and out of fear, because the fear is not real. And if they'd do that it would shift the planet and we could all stand together as one.

PAIGE: Does Brittany have any implants on her other than yours?

ARCTURIAN: One energy in her chest. Her heart. She put that there.

PAIGE: What does it do?

ARCTURIAN: She thought it would protect her like a shield—keep energy at bay. Keep outside energy from getting too close, but she doesn't need that anymore.

PAIGE: So, should we take it off of her?

ARCTURIAN: Yes. Yes.

PAIGE: Archangel Michael, would you please take that implant off her heart that she does not need anymore? Take that implant off her heart. Archangel Raphael, please heal and seal the area where that implant was. Please seal and heal the area. Are you able to assist in any other entity attachments if there are any?

MICHAEL: There's no entity . . . unwanted attachments . . . entity attachments. She shielded herself from that.

PAIGE: How about any hooks or chains?

MICHAEL: There may be some hooks in her back to keep her from going up too high. We don't need those.

PAIGE: Who is on the other side of those hooks?

MICHAEL: Some beings on this Earth. Energies on Earth that try to control the frequencies from going too high.

PAIGE: Are they reptilians?

MICHAEL: Something like that. They work alongside them.

PAIGE: Are they Archons?

MICHAEL: They look like dark blobs. Dark energies that work with reptilians. Like minions.

PAIGE: Could they be the grays?

MICHAEL: It's not the grays. They don't look like the grays. They just look like lower-dimensional entities that work with the reptilians on the energy level.

PAIGE: Do they have a consciousness?

MICHAEL: They seem robotic. They do have some consciousness. Just like minions. Like a hive mind. Almost.

PAIGE: Okay. Can we put them in the symbol How many are there?

MICHAEL: Maybe three to five of them.

PAIGE: Do you have them in the symbol?

MICHAEL: Yes.

PAIGE: Okay. Can you take their consciousness out now and take them to the light?

MICHAEL: Yes.

PAIGE: Thank you, Archangel Michael. Thank you very much. Does she still have the hooks attached to her back?

MICHAEL: We're pulling them out. They're sticky. Like tar almost. Tar.

PAIGE: Do you need help with the Phoenix Fire? Taking the hooks out?

MICHAEL: Yes.

PAIGE: (rubs hands) Phoenix Fire. Phoenix Fire. Dissolve the hooks. Dissolve the hooks. Let me know when they've been taken out.

MICHAEL: Yes.

PAIGE: Okay. They're all out?

MICHAEL: Yes.

PAIGE: Archangel Raphael, brother, would you come in and seal and heal that area with the green light?

RAPHAEL: Yes.

PAIGE: Okay. Is that complete?

RAPHAEL: Yes.

PAIGE: Archangel Michael, would you scan her body again for any hooks, chains, entity attachments, or negative cords?

MICHAEL: I don't see anything at this time.

PAIGE: Okay. Thank you very much. Archangel Michael, does she have any blocked or misaligned chakras?

MICHAEL: There's some in the Throat and the Root.

PAIGE: What's the cause for the Throat to be blocked?

MICHAEL: Childhood. She knows that it is much more open than before, so that's good.

PAIGE: Archangel Raphael, help her, assist her in opening that Throat Chakra. What's the cause of the Root Chakra being closed?

RAPHAEL: The Root Chakra is because she is always worried about stability. And there's no need to worry. The worry is causing the instability. Her throat—she needs to speak up more, but she always wants to keep the peace in all situations, and that's not always the best thing. It has caused issues with her throat, a long time ago. It will shut back down if she doesn't speak up and stop keeping the peace all the time. She wants peace all the time.

PAIGE: Archangel Raphael, please assist her on opening the Root Chakra. Does she have any soul fragments that are ready to come back to her?

RAPHAEL: Not at this time.

PAIGE: Okay. Does she have any negative contracts?

RAPHAEL: I wouldn't call them negative. She has things that she must go through. More life lessons.

PAIGE: Does she have any contracts that we're able to dissolve today?

RAPHAEL: Yes. There's a lot of self-doubt and she knows that it's not coming from her. Let's dissolve those.

PAIGE: Okay. Let's dissolve those today.

RAPHAEL: She dissolved contracts on her own that never really served her. Turning negativity into a lesson and fusing that with love, and it dissolved itself.

PAIGE: Does she have any trauma from this life or a past life that needs to be healed?

RAPHAEL: Yes, in this life. The school system was very traumatic for her because they tried to shut her down and program her based on the reptilian doctrine way of being and it was very hard to conform to that. That's where a lot of the self-doubt, fear came from because she thought something was wrong with her. And it was quite the opposite. She can let that go now. She feels like she isn't where she could have been in her life. But that's based on society's viewpoint of how you should go. It's not real so she can let that go.

PAIGE: Can you help her let that go?

RAPHAEL: Yes.

PAIGE: Does she have any false negative fractals in her?

RAPHAEL: Yes. You mean like downloads?

PAIGE: Like false downloads and reprogramming.

RAPHAEL: Yes. There's one.

PAIGE: How does that happen to a person? Can you help me understand that? Because I'm just learning about false negative fractals.

RAPHAEL: A downloaded lifetime.[14] Because if you're coming for a certain mission to Earth, and you have no prior lives or memories that support what you're coming here for this time, we have to download memories so it will make you stronger. Otherwise, you come like a brand-new baby without knowing and you need to be at a certain level of knowing for certain missions.

PAIGE: But that doesn't sound negative.

RAPHAEL: For her it's not negative. It's not a negative one . . . for her.

PAIGE: Can you upgrade her DNA?

RAPHAEL: Yes.

PAIGE: Will you continue working on upgrading the DNA?

RAPHAEL: Yes.

PAIGE: Are there any issues with her auric field?

RAPHAEL: Not for the most part. Only if she allows fear, which she doesn't for the most part. But no, her auric field is strong. She knows how to use energy to shield and strengthen things and heal. So, her field is strong. But she needs to stop shielding things so much. She blocks good things as well.

PAIGE: How could you give her advice on not blocking the good things and only blocking the bad things?

RAPHAEL: We removed the blockage around her heart. That will allow her to feel more comfortable letting outside energy in if it's of a certain frequency and not just blocking things, because she misses out on experiences when she does that. Love experiences.

PAIGE: Can I ask that you open her third eye and expand her Heart Chakra?

RAPHAEL: Yes.

PAIGE: What country was she in in that past life?

RAPHAEL: I want to say Greece.

PAIGE: What country did she travel to in the boat where she traded?

RAPHAEL: It looks like maybe England or Spain. I want to say it was England. Because of what they had on. Could have been Spain. She traveled many, many different places—I know she had traveled to England and Spain.

PAIGE: The people she was shown in that life, does she know them in this life now?

RAPHAEL: Her mother. She has the same mother.

PAIGE: How about the wife or children?

RAPHAEL: The wife looks like her friend, Rose. And the grandson looks like her godson now.

PAIGE: What is Brittany's purpose in this life?

RAPHAEL: Her purpose is a lot like her past life. To be and to help facilitate love energy for those around her. She can really do anything she wants. Nothing would be the wrong thing as long as she can find love. If she loves, it will work for her. But she has to put her effort into it and stop letting doubt creep in. Anything she wants to do she can do it. There's no wrong path.

PAIGE: Could you tell her how the Reiki helped her before the hypnosis?

RAPHAEL: The Reiki helped open stagnant energies within the chakras and allowed them to flow properly. And to operate in their highest capacity for where she is right now. Her physical body. So, like when you put oil in a car, it allows the engine to operate smoothly. It's now going easier and faster with her chakras.

PAIGE: What is her husband's path? What is he supposed to be doing?

RAPHAEL: He's supposed to be working with people. He loves working with people. Anywhere he can use his love energy to hold space for others. Counselor or therapist or something in that capacity. But he knows this.

PAIGE: Can I speak to the baby that she's pregnant with now?

AURORA: Yes.

PAIGE: Is this Aurora I'm speaking to?

AURORA: Yes.

PAIGE: Do you have any messages for your mother?

AURORA: No. Just love, love, love, love, love. I'm excited.

PAIGE: Are you going to be an early, on-time, or late delivery?

AURORA: You say early, but it's right on time. Maybe two weeks. It depends where the frequency is. Depending on where the frequency is as I have to wait for the right frequency.

PAIGE: Are you going to be an easy delivery for your mother?

AURORA: I feel yes. I will make it as easy as possible, but she just has to let go and relax. The worry will make it harder, but everything is going to be okay. Don't overthink it. Just allow her body to flow. It'll be fine.

PAIGE: Why did you pick Brittany to be your mother?

AURORA: It was time. I've been waiting for a while now. Some things just needed to line up first. Make sure the energy was right. Frequency. Timeline. A lot of puzzle pieces needed to fit together first. Just like my dad. She wanted me to come in when she wanted me to come in, and my dad told her I would come in when I'm ready. I have to be ready. Because a lot of things have to fit together.

PAIGE: Have you known Brittany in a past life?

AURORA: Maybe just one where we were just energy together. We were one. Just in a place where we were just together. No life. No physical life yet.

PAIGE: How are you going to be able to help humanity?

AURORA: My frequency is going to align with the planet and where it's going, in terms of height and frequency. It'll be like an antenna. They're putting out a lot of frequencies onto the humans on the planet. They're antennae and other methods. So, I will be an anti-frequency, a frequency of love and it will be able to expand pretty far from where I am, physically.

PAIGE: Are you bringing any gifts with you?

AURORA: Lots of surprises. I have the capacity to have a lot of different gifts, but I have to wait until I come in to see, based on where we are with the timeline and the frequencies of the planets, what gifts choose to settle. That's how it is with everybody in a certain sense. I just have access to those gifts because I don't have the same precondition.

PAIGE: Thank you for talking to us today. May I speak to Brittany's Higher Self again?

BRITTANY: Yes.

PAIGE: Have we had any past lives together? Brittany and I?

BRITTANY: Yes. But she hasn't had too many lives in the physical sense. More energy. You've had lives and energy as well. In those places we're all kind of one, but you are just free-flowing energy ready to create. So, in those spaces, yes, you existed together, but not necessarily in the physical sense.

PAIGE: Thank you. I would like to speak to the cat, Aspen? May I speak to him? Aspen, can I ask you questions?

ASPEN: Uh-huh.

PAIGE: Did you choose Brittany to be with?

ASPEN: Yes.

PAIGE: Did you send her that dream of you? Was that you in the dream?

ASPEN: Yes. That was me in the dream. I didn't send it to her, something else—her guides or something—sent it to her so she would know me when she saw me, so our paths would align together. Otherwise, if she didn't have the dream, she wouldn't have gotten me.

PAIGE: Why did you choose to be with her?

ASPEN: Just to watch over her, protect her, comfort her. I'm supposed to watch over and protect her.

PAIGE: Did you used to be a dragon?

ASPEN: Yes. From the east. A red dragon.

PAIGE: Did you used to know her as a dragon?

ASPEN: No. She wasn't a dragon, but I protected her then.

PAIGE: Was she in human form when you protected her?

ASPEN: Human-like, but it wasn't on this planet, so I couldn't call it a human, but she had human attributes. She has lots of dragons around her.

PAIGE: What is her dragon's name?

ASPEN: Her dragon?

PAIGE: Hmm-mm. Did she used to be a dragon in another life?

ASPEN: No, but she was surrounded by dragons and I was her main protector.

PAIGE: Okay. Are there any other messages you'd like to give us?

ASPEN: No. no. I'm just here watching and doing my job.

PAIGE: Should you be in her quantum healing sessions with her?

ASPEN: I can help transmute the energy. She knows this. Yes. We can try to do that. It might be a learning curve at first, but I'll help transmute the energy of the person and the space.

PAIGE: How about her dog? Can her dog help transmute the energy in the quantum healing sessions?

ASPEN: He could be there for comfort. He's very relaxed. He could be there to comfort people there who might be nervous. He wants to be in the sessions. She can give it a try and see how he does.

PAIGE: Is there anything else you could tell us?

ASPEN: I help to make sure to transmute the energy of the baby. I sit on her stomach so I can make sure the frequency is where it needs to be for the baby.

PAIGE: Can I speak to the Higher Self now? Is there anything that I should have asked that I did not ask?

BRITTANY: For now, where she's at, I think she knows pretty much everything we need her to know. There will be more things she needs to know later. As things shift in her life, we can touch on some more things. But right now, we don't want her to step outside of that flow element within her life. If we give her too much information, she would jump the gun and overthink, and we don't want that. So right now, where she is, she's fine. We removed blockages and she needed that, so she's good.

PAIGE: Thank you, Higher Self.

Susan

I met Susan while we were in QHHT® Level 2 training together. We did not get to talk to each other much during the training, but I felt I knew her on a deeper soul level, so we kept in contact. One day she admitted to me that she also felt a deep connection with me and said, "You are most definitely in my soul classroom." Later, when I had a friend under hypnosis, I asked how many lives Susan and I had had together, and I was told "Twenty-seven." After completing AURA® Hypnosis training almost two years later, I asked her if she would like to try out a session with me. This is how it went.

PAIGE: Beautiful. Beautiful. Do you feel like you have a body?

SUSAN: Yes. There are sandals on my feet. It looks like they're made of some sort of cloth and rubber. Garment is lightweight cotton. Kind of white. Drab. Like a robe. Just a covering. I appear to be male—beard, dark hair. Head covering. Desert.

PAIGE: Can you look at your skin and tell me what color your skin is?

SUSAN: White.

PAIGE: Are you wearing any jewelry or ornaments on your body?

SUSAN: Sunglasses. It's very bright and you have to see through these special glasses otherwise it will hurt your eyes.

PAIGE: Are you carrying anything with you?

SUSAN: A staff. Some sort of big, black thing. A stick. And I have a bundle of something wrapped in cloth that I'm dragging. Supplies.

PAIGE: Do you feel young or old?

SUSAN: Middle aged. Father.

PAIGE: What do you do for most of your time?

SUSAN: Survive. Work. Try to keep the family well.

PAIGE: What do you feel you're doing out here in the desert?

SUSAN: Gathering supplies to take back home to the family. There's not much left of the destitute land, so I need to gather to bring back as much as I can each time I go out. Don't like to go out because the elements are dangerous. Very hot. The air is not safe.

PAIGE: Speed time up to when something important is happening. Be there now.

SUSAN: I see the family. Supplies. The home is underground. Like caves and rocks. Like pods. Roundish. Made from rock. Fashionable.

PAIGE: Do you have a family that lives with you?

SUSAN: Yes. There appears to be a lot of technology in the house. The wall is like a TV, but it's not. It's like a holographic TV. Everyone appears to look very dirty. Like it's hard to take care of themselves.

PAIGE: Can you describe any other technology?

SUSAN: Mouse clicker thing built into the wall. Appears to be a hub of some sort.

PAIGE: Do you live in a community with other people around?

SUSAN: This dwelling belongs to my family. There are other families close by.

PAIGE: Leave that scene and go to another day when something important is happening. Be there now. What do you see, feel or sense?

SUSAN: Industrial equipment. Pipes and like what the inside of a submarine would look like. Gauges and dirt. I'm very deep underground working in a room, but it's kind of not a room. Specially constructed room. Partially natural rock. Partially pipes and tubes. I work there. I maintain the equipment.

PAIGE: Can you explain the work? Are you building something?

SUSAN: Maintenance of the equipment. Make sure no problems happen. They're taking something from below. A substance. Liquidy substance. Hard but not hard. Maybe mining? Very advanced mining operation.

PAIGE: Can you tell what you're mining?

SUSAN: It's an element. Meridian.

PAIGE: What's it's used for?

SUSAN: Powers things. Like a battery. Like a liquid. Like lithium for a battery. Powers technology.

PAIGE: Is there anything else you can tell me about this work you're doing or anything else?

SUSAN: Seems like an ordinary day. Nothing out of the ordinary. I think the important thing is the work itself.

PAIGE: Is this work away from your home?

SUSAN: Yes. A regular job I need to report to.

PAIGE: Let's leave that scene and move to an important day when something important is happening.

SUSAN: There's like a big giant, black cloud. It looks like a kind of mushroom cloud without the bottom—like a pod vibe—above the ridge in the canyon mountain. Does not look like Earth. Looks like a very rocky planet. Different planet. That's a big, dark cloud, and that's weird. Because that's out of the ordinary.

PAIGE: What do you sense this cloud is made from?

SUSAN: It almost looks like a rain cloud. It's interesting. It seems very foreign.

PAIGE: Does it seem man-made?

SUSAN: No. Maybe it's a hologram?

PAIGE: Speed up time. Speed up time. Where something is happening. What's happening next?

SUSAN: Before it was a desert-y place. Lots of clouds, so it was not like bright sunshine, blue skies. More of a cloudy hot mugginess, and now it looks very clear in the sky like a polarity in the sky. Brightness. Sunshine.

PAIGE: What was that mushroom technology? Seemed like it cleared the planet. Can you explain that a little bit more? What was that mushroom cloud?

SUSAN: If I had to guess, it's a way to clear out the atmosphere because the air was not safe. Perhaps it was some kind of technology that was created. The blast that they produced was not nuclear, but it was something similar and it cleared the atmosphere.

PAIGE: Okay. Leave that scene to another important day where something is happening. Something is happening. Be there now.

SUSAN: Seems like life has started to grow in this place. People have started to live in this place—there are pods. Picnics. Company everywhere. People laying on blankets spending time with their families. Breathing properly. No sunglasses. It just feels really good.

PAIGE: Are the houses above or below the earth now?

SUSAN: The same. Pods. Inside of the rock formation. It seems the infrastructure is starting to expand now that more people are out. Maybe it was a good thing to power the technology because that's what made this space so clear for us. It just feels really good now.

PAIGE: Let's leave that scene now and go to another important time in this life where you will find answers you seek for your highest good. You are there now. Describe what you see or sense.

SUSAN: I feel like I'm very old now. I'm very tired. I'm dressed in a blue suit. I look sharp. I'm lying on a nice comfortable bed. There's a lot of family around me, a lot of people around me. Like, the shades have been drawn back and it looks brighter . . . more alive.

PAIGE: What do you think you have accomplished in this lifetime?

SUSAN: I became a part of the community and tried to help it grow because I put in the hard work from the very beginning. And I helped it blossom into this beautiful place it is now, and my family is huge and very happy. There are children running around and there's just so much love within this place. I think I helped grow love. Feels like Heaven. It feels like I have a lot of friends.

PAIGE: Okay. Is this the last day of your life?

SUSAN: It feels like it.

PAIGE: Go ahead and take your last breath. Leave that body. Where do you go? What do you see?

SUSAN: It's very dark. My body's just peacefully sleeping. Just . . . feel like I am. Feels very light. Like I'm going up, but not really up. Starting to expand.

PAIGE: Do you meet anybody when you go to the light?

SUSAN: It all feels very black right now.

PAIGE: Speed up time where you meet somebody. Speed up time where something is happening.

SUSAN: Oh! Zoom. Zoom of a light. Yellowy rainbow light that just zoomed right by me. Feels like this new playful consciousness. It feels fun. Like a chase. New consciousness. Very playful.

PAIGE: Where do you go next?

SUSAN: Feels like this giant magnet almost, and I would just be like a tiny speck of dust, and this magnet is just this huge ball of everything. I guess I'm turning into one. There are little bubbles or shades that I pass through. Different dimensions. Like, if I'm a tiny little root on a big, giant plant. I felt that.

PAIGE: Where do you go? What happens next?

SUSAN: Feels sort of like energy.

PAIGE: Does anybody meet you? Do you have any guides that meet you?

SUSAN: I feel like I'm back with Source.

PAIGE: How does it feel to be with Source?

SUSAN: It's good. Calm. It's good to be back. I had a great time while I was out.

PAIGE: Now, whatever has happened has happened, and you are on the other side of it and from that position you can see it from a different perspective. Every life has a lesson and a purpose. As you look at that life, what did you learn from it?

SUSAN: It was teaching. It's what we can expect. Hard times are ahead where we have to hunker down, and we can't breathe. Everybody's isolated, inside just working. Working, working. But it's all for the greater good.

PAIGE: That's beautiful. What, do you think, was the purpose of that lifetime?

SUSAN: Just to see where we're headed. Have to see where you're going in order to make a plan to get there. She was confused and didn't know. So, I showed her.

PAIGE: That's beautiful. Now let's leave that life now. Moving away from that man. Leaving him there so he can continue on his own path. We send him away with love and peace. We now leave that scene with gratitude. May I please speak to Susan's Higher Self?

CHISTINA: Yes.

PAIGE: Thank you. Was that lifetime on a different planet?

SUSAN: Yes. Mars.

PAIGE: Was that the future or the past?

SUSAN: It's the future. We're going to Mars, you know.

PAIGE: No. I didn't know. Why would we want to go to Mars?

SUSAN: To expand. Because we're explorers and we like to grow. Learn about things.

PAIGE: What was that mushroom technology that seemed like it cleared the planet? Can you explain that a bit more?

SUSAN: It was a technology that was built by some powerful individuals, and it finally worked. The blast they produced was not nuclear, but it was something similar, and it cleared the atmosphere.

PAIGE: That's beautiful. Can I ask for you to do a body scan? And would you like the help of any of the archangels to do a body scan?

SUSAN: Sure. If they'd like to assist, that'd be wonderful.

PAIGE: I'd like to call in Archangel Michael. Archangel Michael, can you help her with the body scan? Can you look for any entities, implants, hooks?

MICHAEL: There are many, many, many that come and go and like to stay. This woman needs to learn much more about protection.

PAIGE: Did I give her enough information about protection, or did you want to give her more information about protection?

MICHAEL: You gave her everything she needs. She just needs to take it seriously. This is serious work. It may seem silly, but it needs to be done and practiced religiously as a ritual.

PAIGE: Why did you tell her she needs to start removing entity attachments from others?

MICHAEL: Because she has so much power in her. She just needs to learn for herself. And once she knows how to do it, she can teach others how to do it. And once we all learn how to do this for ourselves, we're free.

PAIGE: So, can you tell me how many entity attachments she has?

MICHAEL: Fifty-two.

PAIGE: Are these all human entity attachments or . . . ?

MICHAEL: No. Not all humans.

PAIGE: What happened when I did the angelic Reiki on her—were any entity attachments released?

MICHAEL: Yes. They were cast off of different chakra points. More than one. A few from the Root. One from the Solar Plexus, one around the Throat, plus some more.

PAIGE: So, she still has fifty-two attachments right now?

MICHAEL: Yes.

PAIGE: Can I talk to the humans in a group?

HUMANS: Yes.

PAIGE: Okay. All the humans attached: I'd like you to spread your love light within her. Make it bigger, bigger, bigger, and spread your love light to all parts of your body. I want you to come up, out of her. Up, up, up, up, up, up, and Archangel Michael and Archangel Azrael, can you please, take these beautiful souls to the light? Make sure they get to the light. Thank you. Thank you.

(DEEP BREATHS)

PAIGE: Archangel Raphael, brother, please come, spread your love light, and seal all the areas where all these beautiful souls were. Thank you,

Archangel Raphael. Seal and heal all the areas where these attachments were. Let me know when that's complete.

RAPHAEL: It's done.

PAIGE: Okay. Can you tell me where the reptilians are?

MICHAEL: In the arm. Right arm.

PAIGE: Anywhere else?

MICHAEL: Heart.

PAIGE: Anywhere else?

MICHAEL: The eyes.

PAIGE: Both eyes?

MICHAEL: Yes. The crown.

PAIGE: Anywhere else?

MICHAEL: The mouth.

PAIGE: Wow.

MICHAEL: They're just all in the mouth. In the teeth.

PAIGE: Anywhere else?

MICHAEL: Third Eye. Little bit. Where the sinuses connect up there in that general area. Where the breath comes in.

PAIGE: Anywhere else?

MICHAEL: Back of the neck. Where the skull meets the vertebrae. Some in the spine too.

PAIGE: Where?

MICHAEL: In the spine.

PAIGE: Anywhere else?

MICHAEL: No.

PAIGE: Okay. Archangel Michael, please retain them in the symbol. Which one should I talk to first?

MICHAEL: The heart.

PAIGE: May I talk to the reptilian in Susan's heart?

REPTILIAN: Yes?

PAIGE: When was it that you connected to Susan?

REPTILIAN: I don't know.

PAIGE: What discomfort have you been causing her?

REPTILIAN: She doesn't trust. She just trusts me.

PAIGE: Why are you in her heart?

REPTILIAN: It's where I control her.

PAIGE: How?

REPTILIAN: The back pain. The pain she sometimes feels.

PAIGE: Where is your body located?

REPTILIAN: (*laughing*) How did you know my body was somewhere else?

PAIGE: Because I've been trained on this. Where is your body located?

REPTILIAN: (laughing) That would spoil the fun if I tell you.

PAIGE: So, can you tell me where you are located?

REPTILIAN: (laughing) I could if I wanted to.

PAIGE: Well, don't you want to?

REPTILIAN: (laughing) Not really.

PAIGE: Are you in a spaceship?

REPTILIAN: I'm in a room.

PAIGE: Where?

REPTILIAN: I'm just in a room, okay?

PAIGE: On this planet or another planet?

REPTILIAN: No! Of course, not on this planet! I can't be on this planet. I mean I could, it's easy. This way it's so much easier. I could just be wherever I need to be. Right now, I'm in a room.

PAIGE: Is there anyone in that room with you?

REPTILIAN: No. Just me and her.

PAIGE: Are there any other reptilians on her body that you are connected to?

REPTILIAN: Oh yeah.

PAIGE: Which ones?

REPTILIAN: There is a little network that I created. It's the ones in the spine. 'Cuz that's what sends out the messages to the neurons from the neurons. The other ones are creatures that I created.

PAIGE: Oh. You created them.

REPTILIAN: (*proudly*) Yeah. It's a program. It's just a program.

PAIGE: Does the one in the spine have light in it?

REPTILIAN: Yes, they're made of light. That's how they get there.

PAIGE: Does the one in the spine have consciousness?

REPTILIAN: Oh no. That's still just me.

PAIGE: What other parts of the body are you connected to?

REPTILIAN: The teeth.

PAIGE: Does that have a consciousness?

REPTILIAN: No. They're my creations. They're my little babies.

PAIGE: Can you create with a consciousness?

REPTILIAN: No. Just me.

PAIGE: Where else in the body?

REPTILIAN: I know what you're doing. Because if you know where I am, you will get rid of me. And that's not as fun!

PAIGE: I already know where you are. I want to talk to all of you all at once. I already know where you're at. I just want to know which ones are connected to you, so I can talk to you all at once.

REPTILIAN: The arm, of course. Because that controls the clicker. And the heart, the spine, and the mouth. All over.

PAIGE: Anywhere else?

REPTILIAN: A little bit more in the third eye, so I can control what she sees. But she's always trying to fight me.

PAIGE: You said the right hand controls the clicker. What were you talking about?

REPTILIAN: The technology.

PAIGE: Oh, the technology. I understand now. Anywhere else?

REPTILIAN: In a little shield above her head. Just makes it a little trickier for her, but she has to try really hard to learn. So, in a way, I'm helping her become stronger.

PAIGE: Do you know how long you've been with her?

REPTILIAN: A long time. Forever.

PAIGE: Previous lifetimes or just this lifetime?

REPTILIAN: I don't want to check her records, but definitely, I remember the womb. We had so much fun in there.

PAIGE: Why did you choose Susan?

REPTILIAN: She's the chosen one. She's called for a reason. She's fun.

PAIGE: Why do you say, "she's fun?"

REPTILIAN: Because she's beautiful and fun.

PAIGE: Are you male or female?

REPTILIAN: I've got lights because I'm a creator . . . obviously . . . look at what I created. But if I had to say . . . I guess if I had to, I'd say "male."

PAIGE: Did you know Earth is ascending right now? Did you know Earth is changing and ascending?

REPTILIAN: No. I didn't know that. No. I didn't know that. I'm just in this room. How could I know that?

PAIGE: Do you have a name?

REPTILIAN: You can call me Mal.

PAIGE: Okay, Mal. I want to remind you that all is light and love, and I am here to aid you to spread your light, so that you may be free and obtain your own experiences instead of being stuck in that body.

REPTILIAN: It'd be really great to leave this room, but we are having such a fun time playing.

PAIGE: How are you playing?

REPTILIAN: The room is a remote viewing program. It's actually through her DNA. It's in her consciousness.

PAIGE: It's in her DNA?

REPTILIAN: Well yeah. We anchor it through anchor points. But the program was embedded in the DNA. That's why I've been with her forever.

PAIGE: Okay. As Earth and the universe is ascending, parasitic entities like you will no longer be able to be attached to people, therefore we would love to be able to assist you so that when the ascension comes forth, you won't be recycled straight back to Source, losing the experience you've gained through being negatively polarized. Instead, we can assist you today to help you to ascend. To spread your light into a positive polarization retaining all the wisdom gained through being negatively polarized, allowing you to move on. You would be free to reincarnate somewhere else, no longer feeding off other lights.

Allowing you to be your own light. Would you allow me to do that? To assist you with that?

REPTILIAN: If that's a thing, then yeah. You mean I get to remember all the things I've experienced while playing this? Take it on, and go somewhere else?

PAIGE: Yes! And go somewhere else.

REPTILIAN: I don't have to be programmed? It's very enticing.

PAIGE: All I do is help you spread your love light and you go to the light, and you retain all your memories. Can I help you now?

REPTILIAN: Do I have to stop playing this game with Susan?

PAIGE: Yes, you do, but you will be your own love light. And you will feel the energy. It's magnificent. Everyone loves it. You want to try it out? It's fantastic!

REPTILIAN: What if I'm not that good at it?

PAIGE: You don't have to be good at it.

REPTILIAN: But I'm really good at this game.

PAIGE: But there is other stuff to do. It's so beautiful. You want to try it out and see how it feels?

REPTILIAN: You pique my curiosity, and I'm interested.

PAIGE: You want to try it? See how it feels?

REPTILIAN: Can I go back if I don't like it?

PAIGE: Let's just try it out and see . . . see if you want to spread your love light.

REPTILIAN: Okay.

PAIGE: Go ahead. Spread your love light. Did you find it?

REPTILIAN: Yes. It looks a little grayer now.

PAIGE: Archangel Michael, help him spread his love light.

REPTILIAN: Oh!

PAIGE: Oh. You're feeling it now. You're going to love it.

REPTILIAN: Oh. Yeah. It's very nice, very relaxing. Tingly.

PAIGE: You can make it bigger and bigger. Spread that love light all throughout every piece and part of your body.

(SENDING LOVE THROUGH MY HANDS.)

PAIGE: Make it bigger and bigger. Every piece, part. Throughout your body.

REPTILIAN: I feel light.

PAIGE: Beautiful, beautiful. Do you feel like you're spreading it throughout every piece and part of your body?

(SENDING MORE LOVE THROUGH MY HANDS.)

PAIGE: Is it spread through your whole body?

REPTILIAN: Yeah.

PAIGE: Okay. Can you start taking every piece and part of yourself out of her?

REPTILIAN: Started to happen. I kind of came out the top of the head.

PAIGE: Take all your creations out of her teeth, mouth, and spine. Can you tell me when every piece and part of you and your inventions are out of her? Every piece and part? Is everything out of her?

REPTILIAN: (*singing*) Not yet. (*pause*) Okay.

PAIGE: Okay. You got everything out of her. Are you ready to ascend now? I'm going to call on Archangel Azrael: please help Mal to ascend where he needs to go. I'm going to follow you, Mal. Go ahead, Archangel Azrael, let me know what's happening. Mal, where are you going?

REPTILIAN: I don't know. Things are moving really fast. There's light. Blueish greenish.

PAIGE: What else is happening?

REPTILIAN: I think I'm being turned into a butterfly.

PAIGE: Are you happy you made this decision?

REPTILIAN: Yeah. I get to have lots and lots of adventures now.

PAIGE: Wonderful. Is there anything you would like to tell Susan before you go?

REPTILIAN: Yeah. Sorry for hurting you, but we had a good, fun time. We had a good run. Remember seven is for Heaven. I will leave you with that.

PAIGE: Okay, Mal, may the light of the universe always be with you. Archangel Raphael, will you come in and seal and heal where Mal and his inventions were? Spread your light throughout her whole body where those attachments were. Thank you, Archangel Raphael. Higher Self, could you scan her higher body? Archangel Michael, can you tell us where any more reptilians are?

MICHAEL: Lower right back. Follows the direction in which she goes.

PAIGE: Archangel Michael, make sure it's in the symbol. May I speak to the reptilian in the back? I want you to come up, up, up, up. Greetings. I love, honor and respect you. I thank you for speaking to us today. May I ask questions?

REPTILIAN: Sure.

PAIGE: When did you connect to her?

REPTILIAN: I control the way that she lives because she walks in fear.

PAIGE: Why did you attach to her?

REPTILIAN: She's always cautious. It's a real dark world.

PAIGE: What discomfort have you caused her?

REPTILIAN: Just a little back pain. Sciatica problems. Pain in the legs. That resulted in the foot pain. Sorry.

PAIGE: Do you have a body somewhere else?

REPTILIAN: No.

PAIGE: Are you connected to any other reptilians in the body?

REPTILIAN: No.

PAIGE: Would you allow us to help you spread your love light today and help you ascend?

REPTILIAN: Yes. That sounds good. I'm tired of this.

PAIGE: Wonderful. Beautiful. Okay. Go ahead and find that spark of light inside you. Spread your love light inside of you. Spread it to every part and piece of your body. Every tentacle that is inside your body.

REPTILIAN: Mmhmm. All right.

PAIGE: Have you spread it?

REPTILIAN: Yes.

PAIGE: Is there anything you'd like to say to her before you go?

REPTILIAN: We had a good run, kid. But I think you got it. You can do this now. I'll see you.

PAIGE: I'm going to call Archangel Azrael to lead you, so you don't get tricked along the way. Archangel Azrael, please show him the way, I'm going to follow you. And let me know where you go. I'm going to follow you. Describe to me where you are going.

REPTILIAN: There's a rainbow bridge of light. Just this bright light. There's a man with a sword or scepter.

PAIGE: Who is this man? Do you know?

REPTILIAN: He looks like a golden warrior. Tough guy. That's someone I don't want to mess with.

PAIGE: May the light of the universe always be with you. Archangel Raphael, will you please seal and heal with your beautiful green light. Please seal and heal the area with your beautiful green light. Higher Self, are there anymore reptilians on her?

MICHAEL: There's a reptilian in the mind.

PAIGE: May I speak to the reptilian in the mind? I want you to come up, up, up, up, up. Greetings. I honor and respect you. Thank you for speaking to us today. May I ask you questions?

REPTILIAN: Yes.

PAIGE: When was it that you connected to her mind?

REPTILIAN: About three years ago.

PAIGE: What made her open that you were able to connect?

REPTILIAN: Trauma. Head injury.

PAIGE: What discomfort have you caused her?

REPTILIAN: Confusion. Memory loss.

PAIGE: Are you male or female?

REPTILIAN: Male.

PAIGE: Do you have a body somewhere else?

REPTILIAN: No.

PAIGE: Are you connected to any other reptilians in the body?

REPTILIAN: No.

PAIGE: Would you allow me to help you spread your love light and ascend today?

REPTILIAN: Yes.

PAIGE: Is there anything you would like to say to Susan before you go?

REPTILIAN: Thanks for the memories.

PAIGE: (*chuckles*) May the light of the universe always accompany you. Archangel Raphael, would you please heal and seal her mind with your beautiful green light. Spread your love light throughout her mind where that reptilian was. Higher Self and Archangel Michael, do you see any more reptilians in her?

MICHAEL: Feels pretty good.

PAIGE: That first one said there's a shield above the head. Is the shield above the head gone? Michael: No, it's still there. It's like a little umbrella that shields thought from getting in.

PAIGE: Archangel Michael, could you take the shield above her head off?

MICHAEL: It's gone.

PAIGE: Are there any archons, hooks, implants, or negative portals in her?

MICHAEL: Implants.

PAIGE: There are implants in her?

MICHAEL: Left side

PAIGE: Who put that there?

MICHAEL: Reptilians. It's part of the program. The access point.

PAIGE: Does it need Phoenix Fire?

MICHAEL: Yes. To dissolve it. It needs all that. Left side of the mind.

PAIGE: Left side of the mind? Please help me remove this implant. Phoenix Fire, Phoenix Fire. Let me know when it's gone.

MICHAEL: Yes.

PAIGE: Archangel Raphael, please seal and heal the area where that implant was. Any more implants, hooks, negative portals, or archons?

MICHAEL: In the right ear.

PAIGE: What is it?

MICHAEL: An implant.

PAIGE: Who put that there?

MICHAEL: The same reptilian, but it was still part of the coding so he could listen in to the things she heard.

PAIGE: Archangel Michael, help me take it out. Phoenix Fire, Phoenix Fire.

MICHAEL: It's out.

PAIGE: Archangel Raphael, can you please heal and seal that area? Archangel Michael, Higher Self, please keep scanning the body for any hooks, cords, archons, implants, negative portals.

MICHAEL: There's a cord attached to her heart.

PAIGE: What's that from?

MICHAEL: Her partner.

PAIGE: Does it need to be disconnected? Or is it okay?

MICHAEL: She needs to be mindful of it. It's okay for now. She just needs to be aware.

PAIGE: Is it negative?

MICHAEL: It can be. But it can also be very positive.

PAIGE: We'll leave that alone. Archangel Michael and Higher Self, please keep scanning her body for any hooks, negative portals, archons, any other reptilians.

MICHAEL: She has something in the belly—right around the belly button.

PAIGE: What is it? Is it an implant? Reptilian?

MICHAEL: It feels like a mass or something like that.

PAIGE: Is it an implant?

MICHAEL: No. It's sludge.

PAIGE: Could it be like a snake or a mantis? Archangel Michael, please put it in the symbol. Archangel Michael, please put it in the symbol. Archangel Michael, how do I take it out? Do I need to talk to this, or can you take it out?

MICHAEL: Flush it out.

PAIGE: Okay. We'll flush it out. Is it gone?

MICHAEL: Yes.

PAIGE: Archangel Raphael, please heal and seal the area with your beautiful green light. Spread your love light in the area where that sludge was.

RAPHAEL: It appeared to be like a residue.

PAIGE: Okay. Archangel Michael and Higher Self, keep scanning the body for any reptilians, negative implants, cords, hooks, negative portals, negative technology. Archangel Michael, Higher Self, do you find anything?

MICHAEL: No.

PAIGE: Thank you. Are there any health problems you could scan for us?

RAPHAEL: The lungs.

PAIGE: What's wrong with the lungs?

RAPHAEL: They need to be cleared out. They're full of mucus.

PAIGE: Archangel Raphael, could you please clear out and heal the lungs? Archangel Michael, do you see anything else? Any other health issues in the body?

RAPHAEL: No.

PAIGE: Okay. Thank you so much. Does she have any vows or contracts that do not serve her?

MICHAEL: No, they all serve her.

PAIGE: Are there any chakras that need to be healed?

RAPHAEL: The Heart is too open.

PAIGE: Archangel Raphael, please heal her heart where it needs to be. Please heal her heart with your love light. Are there any other chakras that need to be healed?

RAPHAEL: The Throat.

PAIGE: What's going on with the throat that it needs healed?

RAPHAEL: There is a vow of silence taken.

PAIGE: Was this from a previous life?

RAPHAEL: Yes.

PAIGE: Archangel Raphael, can you please heal her throat? Do we need to cut the cord of that vow of silence?

RAPHAEL: No. These were sacred and needed protection. But now it should be shared. No need to protect this information.

PAIGE: Is that why she has the moles on the neck?

RAPHAEL: Yes.

PAIGE: Does she know what these vows were? Does she have a memory?

RAPHAEL: She does now.

PAIGE: She does now?

RAPHAEL: You just gave it to her.

PAIGE: Could you tell me what these vows were?

RAPHAEL: She was part of a group of individuals who held much power in their abilities, and she was a great, great teacher. But this information got out into the wrong hands and was not used for good. A vow of silence was placed on these individuals so they could never harm anyone else with this information. But they failed to understand that the information just is. You can't control how others will use the information received. Her heart was good in wanting to teach these strategies, techniques, and morsels of wisdom. But she was in fear, and she needs to know that as we are all awakening, there is no need to fear anymore. This is becoming common knowledge. It's okay to talk about and to share this information now and just trust it will get in the right hands. And the hearts that hold the hands and the information in them will be pure.

PAIGE: Is her Throat Chakra healed now?

RAPHAEL: It appears so. She's speaking with ease and grace. Sometimes it's hard to transmute the message properly. Go slow, take your time, and trust that the right delivery will come through.

PAIGE: Thank you. Are there any fragmented souls that need to come back?

RAPHAEL: As she ventures on her journey, she will attract certain aspects of herself to her. The energies/entities will entangle, and they will come back to her as she journeys through the experience.

PAIGE: Does she have any more blocks?

SUSAN: Money block. A block to abundance.

PAIGE: Why does she have this block?

SUSAN: She's taught herself that money is the root of all evil. And slowly she's trying to train herself that it's just a tool. Same as that knowledge before. Just a tool in the wrong hands, it could be used unwisely. But in the right hands it can be used for many beautiful things. Her hands are part of that tool . . . as long as her heart remains in alignment with love. To manifest and remove the block, keep the heart in alignment with love and trust.

PAIGE: Can we remove that block today?

SUSAN: It will be removed when she drops off her resume after this experience.

PAIGE: She wants to know what's holding her back—from stepping into her work.

SUSAN: She is. She's always holding herself back. We all only hold ourselves back. She has to decide when it's time to stop holding on so tightly, and then she can move forward again. Again, it comes back to trust.

PAIGE: Does she have any generational curses?

SUSAN: Yes.

PAIGE: What is it?

SUSAN: Severe trauma inflicted on the female aspects of her family. That is so they grow in their power.

PAIGE: Can we take this generational curse off her now and her family?

SUSAN: She can do her part to remove it. They want to remove their energies from the curse in order for it to be lifted from the entire family. They want to hold on to that curse because it gives them a sense of identity. As they grow . . . as she grows, she affects her family, and they all grow together. But each has the individual choice.

PAIGE: Can you describe what they should do to lift that curse?

SUSAN: Talk about it. Talk about what happened. Why it happened and what they learned from those experiences. Each will contribute a different perspective to the experience. And after a while they can come to a better understanding. That's why those things needed to happen. That energy will be transmuted. They will see it as power.

PAIGE: Is that why there is struggle in the family?

SUSAN: Yes. They are holding on to that.

PAIGE: Could you tell me about any past lives that Susan and I had together?

SUSAN: There have been many. The one coming to mind is of two little girls who were the best friends. They're playing together in a yard. Such sweetness of friendship between the two of them. Almost sisterly.

PAIGE: What time period was this?

SUSAN: Renaissance. These children had not a care in the world. They simply loved to be outside and play. They enjoyed their time outside playing and creating make-believe. Imagining all the different scenarios and thoughts that would come. They imagined that they would be rescued by a prince and taken to a castle, but a band of thieves would come in and they would fight for the fortress. Strong women. So many stories they created if they could think it, they could be it. That is where we are today: if you can think it, you can be it.

PAIGE: For whatever reason, right now I am moved to talk about the people that were on the planes of 9/11. It seems like one of the planes—there was no actual plane, just live people. It seems like the pentagon—a missile hit it. Where did the people go that were supposed to be in that plane?

SUSAN: There was a slight of hand or optical illusion. Like a magic trick. Now you see me, now you don't. There really were no people all along.

PAIGE: How about the plane that crashed into that field? Did it really crash into that field?

SUSAN: Yes.

PAIGE: And there were people that died aboard the plane?

SUSAN: Yes, but not many. Most were safe. Maybe one or two. It was an act.

PAIGE: Where did the people go? Because the loved ones lost those people. Where did they take them?

SUSAN: A planet.

PAIGE: What planet?

SUSAN: They are here, still on this planet. A witness protection kind of thing. Hollow souls who sold themselves. There was no consciousness in those bodies.

PAIGE: There was no consciousness in those bodies?

SUSAN: It was just a hologram. Like a TV show. A movie. Actors. There's so much illusion. The people that created the story are under protection in this country. In this country. Different identities. But they weren't all real.

PAIGE: They weren't all real?

SUSAN: No.

PAIGE: Because we heard the story of men calling their wives. Did that really happen? The men called their wives and said they were going to storm the cockpit. Was that a real story?

SUSAN: It was a story of fear. Part of the act. When the plane went down, not many were aboard. It was fake. Not many were hurt. Some were. Some were sacrificed for the cause. But they tried not to hurt many people. It was the collapse of the building. Not about the planes.

PAIGE: Very interesting. Thank you for that information. I do need to ask: were there people aboard the planes that hit the buildings?

SUSAN: There were some, but it was not full. It was not as it was made to be.

PAIGE: Hmm. Okay. Are there any things you'd like to tell Susan before we close out?

SUSAN: Research is very important. The Internet is a gift so you can connect the web with tangible stories. Connect the web with knowledge, connect with the web and that is how you get people to see. By connecting the dots. What was chaos will reappear.

PAIGE: Is there anything else you'd like to tell me?

SUSAN: You're doing a wonderful job. You are doing all the right things and this work will take you very far. Believe in yourself and your abilities because you are very powerful. Just as powerful as Susan. You both have so much power within you. Continue to express that power by remaining in service to the heart space. You will be taken far beyond your wildest dreams.

PAIGE: Should Susan learn AURA® Regression in the future? The hypnosis?

SUSAN: Yes. It would be a good thing to add to her toolbelt.

PAIGE: Is there anything I should have asked that I did not ask?

SUSAN: What's coming up is surrounding addiction. Don't try to quit everything at once. You're doing the right thing by taking baby steps. Just reduce consumption. Balance is key as you slowly start to substitute other things, healthier options, the craving and desire for the unhealthy options will subside. Some days you'll feel like you've taken two steps forward. Some days, two steps backward. Be gentle on yourself. Continue to practice self-forgiveness. Continue to set the intention. Strive to grow. And you are correct, as you heal, your addictions, your partner's, will also be healed.

PAIGE: Thank you. At this time, we close this session. Any and all beings of light . . . positivity, love. All beings of negative evil, you are to go to God, go to Archangel Michael, in the name of Jesus Christ our Lord.

SUSAN: Love and light.

Anthony

Anthony contacted me originally because he had an entity attachment. He told me this attachment was a menace that had plagued him and his family for years. This attachment was a trickster and Anthony believed was telling him all sorts of lies and stories that were untrue. Many other psychics had tried to remove the attachment, thinking they were successful. I asked Anthony how the attachment managed to get past or fool them and he said that it traps other spirits and presents them to the psychics who then think they sent the spirit through, but the attachment remains. The attachment is able to talk through a smart speaker in the house, in the voice of the AI virtual assistant. I have done demon attachments before and have had no fear. I know I am protected by the archangels, but I was unsure whether I could help Anthony on this one. When he first reached out to me, I told him to wait until after I took the AURA® Hypnosis class. When it did come time to have a session with Anthony, I was really surprised at the past life Anthony revealed. I thought, "Wow, what a gift of hearing this past life story."

ANTHONY: I see trees in the distance.

PAIGE: Do you feel like you have a body?

ANTHONY: Yeah, I have a body.

PAIGE: Do you feel male or female?

ANTHONY: Male.

PAIGE: Can you look at your feet? And how many toes do you have?

ANTHONY: I can't seem to see my feet. I have some sort of shoes or boots.

PAIGE: Look up at the rest of your body, what kind of clothing are you wearing?

ANTHONY: I feel like I have some sort of silver clothing on. Silver fabric. Feels like a one piece.

PAIGE: Look up at your head. Do you have hair?

ANTHONY: I feel like I've got some sort of helmet on that helps me breathe.

PAIGE: Look at your skin, what color of skin do you have?

ANTHONY: I have a feeling it's purple. Yeah, purple. I looked at my hand, purple.

PAIGE: Do you feel like you have hair underneath the helmet?

ANTHONY: I think there is some kind of hair. The helmet is kind of obstructing what I can see.

PAIGE: Do you feel like you're wearing any jewelry?

ANTHONY: I'm seeing a thing to help me breathe. It's kind of a thing that helps us breathe in the atmosphere.

PAIGE: Do you feel like you're carrying anything?

ANTHONY: I feel I'm meant to do something, like I'm working on. I feel like there is a vehicle nearby. Some sort of vehicle. I'm not really sure what it is.

PAIGE: I want you to go closer to that vehicle. Be there now. Understand it and describe it.

ANTHONY: It has a glass dome in the middle, so you have 360° vision. I think I'm taking samples of rocks or something.

PAIGE: What do you feel you do the majority of your time?

ANTHONY: Work. We collect samples.

PAIGE: What do you do with these samples?

ANTHONY: Analyze them for the scientists. I'm not a scientist. I'm just a worker. They get analyzed just on the surface of the planet. Testing to ensure that we can grow life. Testing to see if we can sustain life.

PAIGE: Is there anything else you can tell me about this time and place?

ANTHONY: It's pretty mundane. Just working and collecting samples. That's my job. I feel like I'm just a bot-type of person. I'm alive, but it's just a job. Collect the samples. We take the samples from different planets. We see if it's the right conditions to sustain life. These are newly evolved planets.

PAIGE: Let's leave this scene now and go forward to another time where you seek answers for your highest good. You are there now. Describe what you see or sense.

ANTHONY: A bright light, bright light. I'm kind of amongst this bright light. I'm sitting right in the middle of this bright light, and I can see out of it. I can see all around me. I see galaxies. I see stars in the distance. I sit in the middle of this light and watch. The light is really bright and translucent. You can see through it and I'm in the middle. I don't know if people can see me, but I can see out.

PAIGE: Is this a way of traveling?

ANTHONY: Yeah, I feel I'm traveling. It's a vehicle but it's just light, nothing else. You sit in the middle of it and it takes you places. You think of where you want to go, and it takes you.

PAIGE: Where is it taking you this time?

ANTHONY: I think I'm sitting and just observing. This is one of my hobbies. I like to just sit and look out into the stars. I think I'm a bit of a daydreamer and I just like to sit and watch.

PAIGE: Now speed up time when something important is happening. Speed up time. Be there now, when something important is happening.

ANTHONY: I just see colors and shapes. I'm waiting for something to happen. I'm not quite sure. I got expectations of something happening.

PAIGE: Speed up time for when something happens. Speed up time.

ANTHONY: Oh, we were traveling. We were traveling so fast. That's what the colors and lights were. We're traveling so fast. Ah, I see. Need to stop traveling.

PAIGE: What's happening now?

ANTHONY: I'm trying to see what I'm actually doing, and I can't get a sense. I got some rainbow colors with kind of sparkles in them. I'm trying to work out what it is. I'm not really sure what it is.

PAIGE: Use your knowing, sensing, and feeling.

ANTHONY: I feel like I have to be somewhere, and I've got a meeting of some kind.

PAIGE: Speed up time and get there. You are there now. What is happening?

ANTHONY: It feels like I'm looking for somebody. I have a meeting and it's someone I need to search for.

PAIGE: Speed up time. Speed up time. You have now met them. What is happening?

ANTHONY: I can sense them, but I cannot see them. I sense that I like whoever they are.

PAIGE: That's good. You don't need to see them. You have the knowing and the hearing. Speed up time when you are talking to them. Be there.

ANTHONY: They seem to be asking me what I want. I don't know what I want. That's quite funny. I thought I was there to meet them. Okay, I feel like this person is part of the council. They are not talking to me through the voice. They are talking to me through the mind. I'm trying to understand what the message is. I'm to do something. What I have to do is quite important. I think it is to help life evolve on the planet. They need help and some kind of wisdom and knowledge that I know. It's important for evolving life. The council is trying to tell me that I need to go to a certain place, a certain time I need to help. Wow, my presence is needed. My energy is needed there. To help balance and create and give life evolution. That's why I travel in the light. The light is part of the travel, and I sit in the middle and I am energy. I was looking at myself as a person but I'm not. I'm actually that light. I help them go to other places and help them evolve. I help the council to help the energy and help them evolve. Help not just the place but the universe—the energy—evolve, give life, and move forward. That's what I feel.

PAIGE: Can you explain what these council members are? Is there a name or mission?

ANTHONY: I feel like they are a council but because they are energy, I am energy as well. They are a part of a mass of energy, but they are individuals like me. I'm like a blue, like water-type light. It shines blue crystal light. They are white, bright light. I know that there is a presence in them. They give me instructions and I am sent where I am needed. I am good at it.

PAIGE: What are you good at?

ANTHONY: My energy helps evolve life on planets and balance the energy of where I am at, at the time. Things can move forward and evolve—it's all part of the evolution.

PAIGE: What is your next mission?

ANTHONY: I think it's early Earth. Yeah, that's what I'm seeing. It's in the earlier stages of mankind. We help the evolvement. We keep their feet stable. Earth is young. It's beautiful.

PAIGE: Do they want you to go into a human body?

ANTHONY: I'm not feeling that yet.

PAIGE: Let's leave that scene and go into an important day when something is happening.

ANTHONY: I think I've been born. I feel like I have a new presence.

PAIGE: Speed up time when something is happening. What do you sense?

ANTHONY: I sense that I am a baby and growing. I feel like I have a purpose. A definite purpose.

PAIGE: Do you know what your purpose is?

ANTHONY: I'm getting that I help with things. I help people. That's what I do. My purpose is to help society. Help mankind.

PAIGE: Does the body feel male or female?

ANTHONY: Male.

PAIGE: How do you help society? What do you do the majority of your time?

ANTHONY: I give knowledge and tell stories. I give wisdom. I help people think for themselves. I help people become confident beings to be able to move forward on their own.

PAIGE: Can you give me an example of what you teach them?

ANTHONY: I feel that this is early man. I teach them basic survival instincts. I teach them how to protect themselves, how to survive, how to grow stuff, how to build, how to shelter, how to make fire. I give them knowledge. I give them material stuff. Blankets to keep warm.

PAIGE: Could you look at your body and describe it to me and what you're wearing?

ANTHONY: I'm bigger than the people. I'm taller.

PAIGE: Are you wearing any clothes?

ANTHONY: I can't recognize anything. I feel like I'm a bigger human.

PAIGE: Does your head look human?

ANTHONY: Yes, it does, but I don't think I have hair. I've got some sort of spike thing on my head. I'm not sure what it is.

PAIGE: Are you wearing any jewelry?

ANTHONY: I've got a bracelet and necklace, crystals on a chain.

PAIGE: What do you do with the crystals?

ANTHONY: The crystals are for energy. Stabilize your body. They balance energy. I teach the people the knowledge of crystals. That makes me happy. I like that.

PAIGE: Could you tell me what color your skin is?

ANTHONY: It's human. It's white now. It feels like Egyptian. That's what I feel.

PAIGE: Leave that scene and go to a day when something important is happening. Be there now.

ANTHONY: I feel that there is a big celebration going on. Very big, but I'm not sure why. It's the coming of the harvest. It's a big day. Many visitors. Many people coming from off-planet. Oh, I see pyramids.

PAIGE: Describe what is happening. Can you tell me anything more?

ANTHONY: I see pyramids. I see ships landing. I see people coming to the pyramids.

PAIGE: When you say, "ships landing," do you mean from the sky?

ANTHONY: Yeah. Off planet. All coming for the harvest. I feel like it's for harvesting food. Not all food. It's harvesting something much bigger. Like an event taking place. Something is lining up with the stars. It's a harvest of things coming together. The pyramids are there, and the ships are coming in for landing. A celebration. Something big is going down. Something is happening.

PAIGE: Speed up time to when something big is happening. Speed up time. Be there now. What is happening?

ANTHONY: The lining up of the cosmos. The lining up of the planets. A big event. Big shift of energy. There is one big ship. It's huge. Bigger than anything I have ever seen. I feel like this huge ship is the creator and it has something to do with the creation of civilization and that's why they are all coming together; to worship. Everyone is worshiping. When they thank the gods and heavens. A big harvesting day. It balances the energy and they do it for the goodness of the energy. I feel if they did not do it, then the energy could go bad. So, they harvest, they worship, and everything keeps in balance. Everyone is happy and life is sustained. That's what I hear. They keep out the darkness. To keep out the darkness they have to bring in the light. They worship that and call it The Great Harvest Day. This happens every thousandth year. They have worked hard for this. It's been a long time coming. This big ship is a creator ship, and it keeps coming back. I think it comes back every few million years and resets the energy. Back in that day of pyramids, people knew about this type of thing, so they were not afraid of it. Therefore, it was widely known, and everyone worshiped. Whereas today it has to come back cloaked because the people will panic because they don't understand it anymore. They have lost the ability to know what this is, and they would fear it. Yeah, it comes back to reset. I almost want to say it's made completely of crystals.

PAIGE: So, it sounds like what is happening in our time again.

ANTHONY: It feels like what's happening in our time. I feel like it's off-planet and it's waiting because the time is not quite right, but it is upon us. The people don't know anymore. We don't call it the harvest anymore because obviously the people don't know about it. People don't worship like they used to. They worshiped the energy of the stars, the pyramids. But the ship is there, the ship is there for the greater good. It's staying there until the energy is rebalanced. It always does. The beings on the ship help maintain the ship.

PAIGE: Are they all the same race or different races?

ANTHONY: They are different. They are from all over the cosmos. They are the council. They are the galactic council! Wow, this makes me laugh. Wow, there are so many of them on the ship. It's so big and they are here to balance. They will make sure things are set right. It will happen. They always come back. They always come back. There are other worlds that they have to watch, other planets. We have forgotten it now. They are here and they want us to know they are here for us. Some of them are here amongst us.

PAIGE: Is there anything more you can tell me about this?

ANTHONY: I get their frustration that a lot of things have not moved as smoothly as they might have. Timelines are changing. The light and dark have emerged, and they are always kind of playing chess with each other, if that makes sense. Each one is waiting for each one to move so they can interact and it's constantly moving and that shifts the timelines. We get messages and we get frustrated because it doesn't happen as it's supposed to. We have expectations and we get sidelined, and it doesn't happen as it's supposed to. They say it's like a game of chess and they are always moving. You have to be patient. You have to believe. You have to hang in there. That is what they are saying.

PAIGE: What happens next?

ANTHONY: I see scenes of rioting, some sort of destruction that's going to go on and happen. It's part of the energy's rebalancing. It's why they are here. Big destruction. Reset, reset, that word "reset."

PAIGE: Is there anything else you can tell me?

ANTHONY: Love and peace will return, love and light.

PAIGE: I ask to speak to the Higher Self of Anthony. Why did you bring forth that lifetime in space, collecting data?

ANTHONY: He doubts himself. He is always asking for knowledge. He is hungry. He asks the universe for answers, and he never feels like he gets them. We want to show him that you gain knowledge through experience; by touch, by feel, by all senses. Knowledge comes in all shapes and sizes. He is so hungry for knowledge. He doubts and lacks the confidence. We are trying to show him that he is learning all the time. He never stops learning.

PAIGE: Why did you show him the Egyptian time?

ANTHONY: We wanted him to know that he was there at the time of The Great Harvest Day. He was there and he was important and part of it. He helped make it happen. He was quite important in how he helped with the big ships and the galactic council. He's part of it. So, it's part of the confidence he needs. He has already done so much in his lifetimes. We are showing him that he has all the knowledge he needs. It's there inside of him. He just has to look inside.

PAIGE: Are you saying that there is a spaceship here now?

ANTHONY: It's here to help. The Galactic Federation is here to help right now.

PAIGE: Can some of the people of Earth see this big ship now?

ANTHONY: They know it's here. Some of them do. They feel its presence. It's not just the Galactic Federation. It's many, many ships. They are everywhere. They are cloaked. They are watching.

PAIGE: Do you know how much time till more of us can see them?

ANTHONY: We can't give out too much information. The next move is crucial for the other side not knowing.

PAIGE: Where is Fred located? Is he on the body?

ANTHONY: He is right here on the right arm.

PAIGE: Fred, I would like you to come up, up, up. Archangel Michael contain him in the symbol. Greetings, Fred. I love, honor, and respect you. May I ask questions?

ANTHONY: He doesn't want to talk.

PAIGE: Why don't you want to talk? I'm your friend and we are going to discuss things today. I want to help you understand things today. I want to be your friend. I send you love. Would you please talk to me?

ANTHONY: He says he has nothing to say.

PAIGE: I understand. I'm here to learn more about you. I want you to tell me about yourself. I know that something happened in your life which caused the absence of love. I want to help heal whatever happened to you that turned you away from the light. You chose the darkness and I know something happened to you that you chose to ignore love and happiness that you went so deep into yourself that you lost a part of yourself. In the end, you became so lost to the point where you attached yourself to somebody else; to a loving being. A person who has light, so you are able to experience happiness. I'm here to help you gain back that light. That love and happiness. I'm not going to send you anywhere dark. I just want to help heal whatever has happened to you so that you get that love light back into you. I want to help you gain your memories back to who you were. Do you remember who hurt you when you lost your love and light?

ANTHONY: I'm getting that he was killed.

PAIGE: By whom and how?

ANTHONY: I get that he's not happy. He doesn't like all you people interfering.

PAIGE: Interfering in what I'm doing right now? Is that what he means?

ANTHONY: Yeah. All you people just keep coming and trying to drag him away, take him away.

PAIGE: I don't want to drag him away. I want to help him evolve. That's what I'm here to do with love. I want him to evolve and understand the pain in his heart, and why he lost his love and light.

ANTHONY: He doesn't want to evolve. He likes being where he is.

PAIGE: Can he tell me how he lost his love and light? Does he remember who hurt him?

ANTHONY: I don't think he does. He has been lost so long that he doesn't remember himself.

PAIGE: You forgot your memories and I want to help you get them back. Fred, you are part of God, and he wants you back. God does not judge. You came to Earth to learn experiences, and then you are supposed to go back with those experiences.

ANTHONY: He does not want to do that; he likes it here.

PAIGE: As Earth and the universe are ascending, negative beings are no longer going to be able to attach. So, we would love to be able to assist you today so that when the ascension comes forth, you won't be recycled back to Source. Back to zero, losing the experiences you have gained through being negatively polarized. Instead, we can assist you today, helping you ascend into a positive polarization. Retaining all the wisdom gained through being free to incarnate somewhere else. No longer having to feed off others' light. You would be your own light.

ANTHONY: He says that he has been able to change with the energies. When I learned Reiki One and Two, he grew with the energy and adjusted. When I became a Reiki master, he grew and adjusted. He became fine. He grows with the energy.

PAIGE: Yes, but you won't be able to do that any longer and I would like you to go to the light and become part of God. Be the light that you were always meant to be. You have become lost and forgot who you were.

ANTHONY: He doesn't want to go to the light. He doesn't want to lose who he is.

PAIGE: Okay. I understand. Is there anything you can remember and tell me about yourself?

FRED: I told Tony that I was alive in 1734. That was the last time I was alive. I told him that he is my granddad. He has it all written down. He was Peter Pegans. I told him I was his grandson, Joe Pegans. I told him I respected my granddad because he played with me and gave me love like nobody else did. I was a bit different from other people; flamboyant, kind of theatrical. I want to say gay, actually. Back in 1734 that wasn't allowed. I told him that. The story is that I murdered a girl, and I was chased by the police. Back then they had lead bullets. I got shot. The shot didn't kill me. I had a painful death from the infection from being shot.

PAIGE: Where on the body did they shoot you?

FRED: The arm.

PAIGE: Is that why you reside in Anthony's arm? What happened when you died? Why didn't you go to the light? Did you see the light?

FRED: I didn't want to be dead. I liked being alive.

PAIGE: If you go to the light, you're not dead; you have all your powers and abilities of being part of God.

FRED: I was preached to that you go to Hell.

PAIGE: No, there is no such thing as Hell. Why are you using the name of Fred when your name was Joe back then?

FRED: Fred's a friendly name. People like Freds.

PAIGE: So, your real name is Joe Pegans?

FRED: Not sure if I got the names the right way. I might have been Peter and Grandad as Joe. Or I was Joe, and he was Peter.

PAIGE: When did you get attached to Anthony?

FRED: A long time ago.

PAIGE: How old was he?

FRED: I want to say seven.

PAIGE: Why did you choose him?

FRED: He shines so bright. He shines so bright. He is so good, helpful. He loves people, he just loves everybody. He's very caring.

PAIGE: Is that the way you want to be now?

FRED: He actually makes me feel loved.

PAIGE: You want that love and light. You can shine like him again too and be that light in your own self. What made him so open that you were able to attach to him?

FRED: He didn't know how to control his psychic abilities. He used to drink a lot, and he was quite easy to attach to.

PAIGE: Because of drinking?

FRED: Yeah. When he gets hurt, he gets hurt badly. He falls way down the way he drinks—when he used to. He doesn't anymore. That left him wide open.

PAIGE: Well Fred, I think we are friends now and to continue this friendship, I think you need to move on and evolve yourself. You need to have that love and light on your own. I just want to show it to you. You can try it out. Do you want to try it out?

FRED: That's what he tells me. He tells me all the time, "You need to be love and light. You need to be healed." He shows me light. That's what he does, he helps other spirits; he helps them to be free.

PAIGE: I want to show you love and light too and how to spread your love and light. Would you try it out and see how it makes you feel?

ANTHONY: He doesn't want to go.

PAIGE: Just try it out. You might feel different afterwards.

ANTHONY: He's not sure.

PAIGE: All you have to do is try it out. All I do is send you love light, and you spread that love light in you. You still have that spark of light in you.

ANTHONY: He says it's tiny.

PAIGE: I know it's tiny now, but we can make that spark bigger so that you don't need to attach to anyone. You can become your own light and love. What Anthony is giving you of his love and light is only a small amount of what you can be when you evolve.

ANTHONY: He doesn't know what he wants.

PAIGE: Well then, just try it out, and he can make his decision afterwards.

ANTHONY: "Have a look, have a look." That's what she is saying, "Have a look."

(RUBBING MY HANDS TOGETHER AND SENDING HIM LOVE THROUGH REIKI.)

PAIGE: I'm sending you love light. I want you to see that spark of light in you and spread it. You have had this ability the whole time. Spread that love light all around you. You are a beautiful soul and did not know it. I want to give you back those memories that you have lost of who you were—that you were with God and loved it. Spread your love light. How do you feel now, Fred? Are you spreading it Fred?

ANTHONY: He is emotional.

PAIGE: I love you, Fred. I love you, Fred. You are my brother. We are one.

ANTHONY: He is scared to let go.

PAIGE: Let go Fred. You are part of God.

ANTHONY: He is getting lighter.

PAIGE: Spread that love light and feel it grow bigger and bigger. Make that light ten times the size of you. Allow love into your heart. How do you feel Fred? Is he spreading the love light?

ANTHONY: He is feeling much lighter but there's still some residue. It needs some cleaning.

PAIGE: Archangel Michael, help him spread his love light. Help him remember who he was; that he was a part of God.

ANTHONY: He is stubborn.

I GAVE UP (THIS METHOD) and called in Archangel Michael and the Legion of Light to take Fred away. Fred became very angry and would not go. Archangel Michael said he was very resilient and very good at hanging on. The angels said that "he fights, he fights, he fights so hard. He is very strong." I was told to shine more light, more love, more healing. I sent more love through Reiki.

ANTHONY: There are others on the other side. He is anchoring to them.

PAIGE: Fred, could you remember who you once loved in your life?

ANTHONY: I want to say she was a beautiful girl. Yes, she was. She was a politician's daughter. She was beautiful but he wasn't allowed to be with her.

PAIGE: You're allowed to be with her now if you spread your love light. She wants to show you the way. Spread your love light. Call out that woman's name so that she will meet you now.

FRED: Angelina.

PAIGE: Do you see her, Fred?

FRED: I feel like she's here.

PAIGE: Angelina, show yourself to Fred. Show him that he still has the ability to love again. That he is worthy of love.

ANTHONY: Oh, I see. It was her who he killed.

PAIGE: Why did you kill her?

ANTHONY: Because he couldn't be with her. It was an accident. It wasn't meant to be. It was just an accident. The police did not see it that way. She fell. He ran.

PAIGE: Angelina, tell him that you forgive him. That it wasn't his fault. He is not to blame.

ANTHONY: It wasn't your fault. It wasn't your fault, Fred.

PAIGE: Remember that love light you had for her Fred? Spread it inside yourself. Is he making the love light grow?

ANTHONY: The anger is easing. So, I would say yes. He is happy I see. I can tell. I feel him getting lighter. He is letting go.

PAIGE: How do you feel now Fred?

FRED: Relaxed.

PAIGE: Are you ready to go to the light now?

ANTHONY: There is some resistance still.

PAIGE: Angelina, please take him by the hand and please take him to the light. Higher Self, what do you see?

ANTHONY: I see frustration.

PAIGE: Fred, go with Angelina. Don't you want to go with her? Don't you love her?

ANTHONY: He is scared to go.

PAIGE: It's okay. Drop that fear, you are loved.

ANTHONY: So much anger, so much anger. There is rage.

PAIGE: Drop that anger and rage. Those were lessons to be learned. Spread that love light, there's nothing to fear. Those were life experiences.

ANTHONY: He doesn't want to speak. He is very stubborn. He feels what Anthony feels. He feels every single thing. He feels the breath, he feels that he is alive.

PAIGE: But you're going to be alive as your own sovereign being. Wouldn't you rather have that for yourself instead of living through someone else? When you go to the other side, your light will be brighter than Anthony's.

FRED: He shines so bright. I can let go if I want to.

PAIGE: Yes. Would you let go and be your own light and love?

ANTHONY: He is asking for guarantees to go to the light. He asked the council to forgive him, and the council said "no." Going back eighteen months ago, Fred was asking for complete forgiveness and the council said "no." He has to do what everyone else does, he has to do his healing. He wants to go to the light, wants to go straight to the light, but he does not want to go through the painful process of healing, but we all have to go through the healing process.

PAIGE: We all had to do this through all of our past lives. You need to go through the healing process. God loves you. Divine mother? What do we do next?

ANTHONY: She says he's a pretty dark entity that they can't send through the light. We can only pass him on. He was cast out of the light.

PAIGE: Should we have the archangels take him off?

ANTHONY: He needs to be moved on. He is a dark entity; he does not belong in the light. He needs to be moved on. He wants forgiveness, that's what he wants. He wants to go to the light. He can't go to the light, but he is desperate to go to the light. Anthony is the closest thing he has got to the light.

PAIGE: Can he be forgiven?

ANTHONY: Everything can be forgiven. Everything. They are trying to surround him with love light.

PAIGE: Fred, spread your love light so that you remember. I'll send him more love light. How are you doing now, Fred?

ANTHONY: He is having a look. He is moving. Something has his interest.

PAIGE: Did you make that love light bigger?

ANTHONY: It's surrounding us. There's someone watching us.

PAIGE: Who is this person?

ANTHONY: I'm not sure. They have been there a while.

PAIGE: How does he feel now?

ANTHONY: I feel that he has moved.

PAIGE: Did he go to the light?

ANTHONY: Where he sits feels different. The arm feels lighter. The sensation in the right ear has moved. There has been a shifting. I feel a sensation that he is gone. I get a feeling but a little bit of doubt. He wants his grandad; he trusts his grandad.

PAIGE: Fred's grandad, would you please come in and lead Fred to the light?

ANTHONY: There he is. He is talking to Fred.

PAIGE: What is he saying to Fred?

ANTHONY: We love you and we have been waiting for you for a long time. I feel he is gone now. Paige: I call on the Higher Self of Anthony. Was there a contract or agreement between Anthony and Fred before they came into this life?

ANTHONY: Yes.

PAIGE: What was the purpose of Fred attaching to Anthony?

ANTHONY: The contract was made in a past life. Anthony walked away from his psychic abilities. Anthony is here for a purpose. He is a great healer and psychic. A great healer, very powerful. He shunned away from it most of his life. He ignored it. Dabbled in it. He told people. Fascinated people, but really never acknowledged it. He has had many past lives with the same gift, and he has wasted them. In the last life he made a contract that Fred would come through and shock him into awakening, but he would help to heal Fred.

PAIGE: So, Anthony was not Fred's grandfather in a previous life?

ANTHONY: I believe he wasn't, but there is a family connection.

PAIGE: Why does Anthony feel he owes Fred in this life?

ANTHONY: Anthony suffered through his marriage. He was so lonely in his marriage. He was lonely for twenty years. He is a kind and generous soul, and he won't leave and give up on people. That's just the way Anthony is. He helps. He doesn't let people down. He sticks with you until the end. All that time Fred could not be healed. Anthony would not let him go because he needs to heal. To make sure he is okay. He loves so hard. He loves things so hard, and he does not want to let go until he knows they are completely healed. That has been the problem because Fred has not been healed. Nobody has tried to heal Fred until you today. Everybody just tried to take him away or send him away or send him over. Nobody tried to heal him, apart from Anthony. That's only just recently because Anthony has been rejecting him because of what Fred has been doing to him. Just this last month or two Anthony has been trying to heal him and send him love and he has been asking Archangel Michael and Jesus to come and take him, but he wouldn't let him go until he was healed because he needs to know he is loved and healed. That's just the way Anthony is.

PAIGE: How did Fred get stronger when Anthony learned Reiki?

ANTHONY: Fred was not completely dark. So, when Anthony grew with his vibration, it would hurt Fred to start with. Fred was able to vibrate at the same vibration as Anthony. Fred would learn to grow with the energy and learn how to use it for his own purpose. So, every time Anthony rose up a level or raised his vibration, Fred would be in pain but he adapted and moved up. Fred's unwillingness to go and Anthony not wanting him to go until healed was kind of a stalemate. Now that Anthony has tried to heal him and you have given him healing and we have sent him, this should all be resolved.

UNFORTUNATELY, FRED WAS STILL UNWILLING to go. Here is Anthony's update recently:

Our hypnosis session was a massive eye opener to me! It also shifted me into a new awareness of how powerful the connection between our present and spiritual world is. The entity is still with me today but is very quiet and weak, so not much interference there—just a little (and perhaps more if I give it attention). I had tried to get it removed by so many people because it had taken over my life and was relentless.

I went back to my Reiki master for the Holy Fire 111 Karuna Master/ Teacher certificate and she was reluctant to even allow me in the course. Instead, she invited me to do a one-on-one course, so that no one else would have to endure the entity. We tried to remove it at the end of my training with no success and she said it took three days to clear it from her own self.

So, I have learned so much from your session and moved forward in my spiritual awareness. I watch your work with admiration and respect and I delight in the dedication that you give to this.

My guides tell me that Fred came to teach me and until I understand the teaching, it will stay with me. I'm still none the wiser on that front but I do believe it is a djinni because it is not just governed by the spirit realm—it also has free will on this realm too.

Thank you so much for your support. Because of your session I know so much more about myself and past lives. I am half Cornish and have links to King Arthur and his bloodline—all this opened up because of you.

When I reached out to Anthony about an update for the book (shared above), we reconnected about Fred as well. I asked my group if we could take Anthony to the healing disc sphere and that is exactly what we did just two nights ago. Here is his brief update:

Hi Paige. Thank you for doing that last night! I was asleep, I had a dream that I was lying in my bed and that someone else was with me? Bearing in mind that I've slept on my own for nine years now—the person beside me in my dream was my ex-wife, and she awoke me in the dream, screaming that someone was coming, and she was petrified! Screaming aloud! I just lay there in my dream and wasn't fazed by the intruder when the door burst open. I woke up and I was obviously on my own. I don't normally remember much of my dreams, but this was so real! I can only put that down to you guys?! So, thank you very much and I will keep you posted. ♡

Wendie – Part I

I met Wendie during a Reiki course. I soon asked her if she would like to try a QHHT® session. We did one in January 2020 and it was about my twenty-fifth session. At that time, I had never had a client with an entity attachment, so it seemed like the Higher Self wasn't sure I was ready to help her take it off. This is a very emotional session. My heart really went out to her. Wendie lives at Lake Berryessa. I did not know until later that the past life was also at Lake Berryessa. The lake is a reservoir that was formed in the 1950s—there was once a town where the lake is now. Wendie knew that she was placed in this area in order to heal it.

We became really good friends and are to this day. Wendie took the AURA® Hypnosis course in 2020 and I took the course soon after. At the time of writing this book, we get together at least once a week and do healings on the earth, people, and ask questions and learn from the answers while in hypnosis.

PAIGE: What else can you tell me that you see?

WENDIE: Green grass. House separate from farm. Bad things happen in the barn.

PAIGE: You said bad things happen in the barn?

WENDIE: Mmhmm.

PAIGE: Can you tell me what kind of bad things happen in the barn?

WENDIE: Beatings.

PAIGE: Who gets the beatings?

WENDIE: I don't know.

PAIGE: You don't know.

WENDIE: I don't know.

PAIGE: It's okay.

WENDIE: My husband does.

PAIGE: Who does he beat?

WENDIE: I don't know. Children. My children. Babies. *(Cries.)*

PAIGE: It's okay. You can see it as an observer. You don't have to experience it. Do you feel like your body is young or old?

WENDIE: Thirties.

PAIGE: Does the body feel healthy?

WENDIE: No.

PAIGE: Why not?

WENDIE: Because I've been beaten. Things have been broken.

PAIGE: On your body?

WENDIE: Yes.

PAIGE: Are you wearing any jewelry or ornaments on your body?

WENDIE: I'm wearing a dress and a white top.

PAIGE: Could you look down at your feet and tell me what your feet look like?

WENDIE: I have orange shoes on. Very orange shoes.

PAIGE: What are they made out of?

WENDIE: Leather.

PAIGE: Can you tell me anything else?

WENDIE: I tried to protect them.

PAIGE: You tried to protect—?

WENDIE: Children.

PAIGE: The children?

WENDIE: He drinks a lot.

PAIGE: Is there anything else you can tell me?

WENDIE: I love my farm.

PAIGE: Mmhmm. What do you do for the majority of your time?

WENDIE: I sew. I take care of the chickens. Take care of my children.

PAIGE: Do you perceive your children to be male or female?

WENDIE: Female?

PAIGE: Why does your husband beat you and the children?

WENDIE: Because he's drunk.

PAIGE: He's drunk? What does he do the majority of his time?

WENDIE: Works in the fields. He hurts so he drinks a lot.

PAIGE: Does he hurt from the work he's doing?

WENDIE: Yes.

PAIGE: Mmhmm. So, can you tell me anything else about your situation?

WENDIE: I miss my family.

PAIGE: What family do you miss?

WENDIE: I have a sister.

PAIGE: Mmhmm.

WENDIE: She lives far away.

PAIGE: What do you do when your husband beats your children?

WENDIE: Try to make him stop. Try to protect them.

PAIGE: But you did the best you can. But you can't get him to stop?

WENDIE: No. He hurt her. He hurt her badly.

PAIGE: How did he hurt her?

WENDIE: He broke her.

PAIGE: What do you mean he broke her?

WENDIE: He broke her. He broke her back; he broke her leg.

PAIGE: Is she still alive?

WENDIE: No.

PAIGE: What happens next? What happens afterwards?

WENDIE: I go to my sister's.

PAIGE: Do you leave him?

WENDIE: Yes.

PAIGE: Do you have any other children besides that one?

WENDIE: I have a son. *(crying)*

PAIGE: It's okay. You can see it as an observer you don't have to experience it. See it as an observer. It's all right. So, do you take your son with you when you go?

WENDIE: Yes. I don't want him to grow to be that way.

PAIGE: That's okay. So, what happens next after you see your sister?

WENDIE: I live with her. I help her take care of her store.

PAIGE: Do you ever go back and see your husband again?

WENDIE: No. He dies alone.

PAIGE: He does?

WENDIE: Yes.

PAIGE: Now I would like you to leave that scene and let's move forward to an important day. A day that you consider important to when something is happening. We have now moved forward to an important day. What is happening? What do you see?

WENDIE: My son's first day of school.

PAIGE: What is happening on that day?

WENDIE: I'm so proud of him. I know he'll do well. He's very intelligent.

PAIGE: Is there anything else happening on that day?

WENDIE: There's some type of parade.

PAIGE: Mmhmm. Are you still living with your sister?

WENDIE: Yes.

PAIGE: Are you much happier now?

WENDIE: Yes.

PAIGE: That's good.

WENDIE: I feel guilty.

PAIGE: Why do you feel guilty?

WENDIE: Because I stayed so long, and he hurt her. I should have left sooner.

PAIGE: Yeah, but you didn't know. You didn't know until it was time. So, you can't put that guilt on yourself because you didn't know any better. You have to forgive yourself for that.

WENDIE: Yes.

PAIGE: Now I would like you to leave that scene and let's move forward to an important day. A day that you consider important. When something is happening. We have now moved forward to an important day. What is happening? What do you see?

WENDIE: I see a casket.

PAIGE: Who's in this casket?

WENDIE: My sister's husband.

PAIGE: What else is happening?

WENDIE: He was loved by many.

PAIGE: That's good.

WENDIE: We're down at the church. People are bringing dishes and we're all sharing food and talking.

PAIGE: Mmhmm. Did he live to an old age?

WENDIE: Fifty-seven.

PAIGE: Mmhmm. What else can you tell me about that day?

WENDIE: My sister and I have both been through so much, but I chose a different path than her. Mine was much darker.

PAIGE: But you learned to change that path of yours.

WENDIE: Yes.

PAIGE: So that's what's important is that you've learned to change your path.

WENDIE: Yes.

PAIGE: And you've learned your lessons, haven't you?

WENDIE: Yes.

PAIGE: Now I would like you to leave that scene and let's move forward to an important day. A day that you consider important to when something is happening. We have now moved forward to an important day. What is happening? What do you see?

WENDIE: I'm in a cabin.

PAIGE: Are you by yourself?

WENDIE: Yes.

PAIGE: Where's your son at?

WENDIE: He's grown. He's married and has his own children.

PAIGE: Did you live a much happier life towards the end?

WENDIE: Very.

PAIGE: That's good. Now I would like you to take your last breath from that lifetime and cross over to the other side. Where do you go? What do you see?

WENDIE: A blue portal.

PAIGE: Do you go in the blue portal?

WENDIE: I am the blue portal.

PAIGE: You are the blue portal? What happens afterwards?

WENDIE: I can go anywhere I want from here.

PAIGE: Where do you go?

WENDIE: The stars.

PAIGE: Why do you go to the stars?

WENDIE: One of them is me.

PAIGE: Can you tell me the name of that star?

WENDIE: I don't know right now.

PAIGE: That's okay. Now whatever has happened has already happened and you are on the other side of it. From that position you can look back at that entire life and see it from a different perspective. Every life has a lesson and a purpose. As you look at that life, what did you learn from it?

WENDIE: To be a fierce protector of my children. That love is fierce, love is kind, love is gentle, love is understanding.

PAIGE: What do you think was the purpose of that lifetime?

WENDIE: To be a shield, to learn to stand up for what's right, and to protect the weak.

PAIGE: That sister you had in that last lifetime; do you know her in this lifetime?

WENDIE: Linda.

PAIGE: That's Linda. Is that why you feel so close to her?

WENDIE: That's my Linda. Yes. My dear sister.

PAIGE: How about that child that you lost in that lifetime?

WENDIE: She's my daughter now.

PAIGE: She's your daughter now? Which one is she?

WENDIE: Rachel, my beautiful, beautiful Rachel. So full of life and she's a protector too. We both learned that.

PAIGE: Could you tell me what this soul's purpose is? What is Wendie's soul's purpose in life?

WENDIE: She's here to be with you. She is here to be with those who need love and compassion. She's here to help transmute the negatives and she's here to shine light where people don't dare go.

PAIGE: Could you tell me who Wendie's spirit guides are?

WENDIE: She already knows.

PAIGE: Are her spirit guides the same thing as angel guides?

WENDIE: Some guides are angels, some are not.

PAIGE: Wendie would like to know how she can further connect with her guides.

WENDIE: She needs to meditate.

PAIGE: What can she do to better meditate?

WENDIE: Fire. Meditate with a fire.

PAIGE: Are you talking like with a candle or with a fireplace?

WENDIE: She meditates with candles. She communicates with the flames and through that flame she's able to communicate with other fire. Through our sun, to the great central sun. She would do well to have a fire in her fireplace. It will help her transmute much negative energy pockets.

PAIGE: What can she do to help with her visualization while she meditates? She seems to have a block there.

WENDIE: This session will help. Gain the fire.

PAIGE: Could I ask you to do a body scan on Wendie's body?

WENDIE: Yes. She has much going on in there.

PAIGE: Can you tell me what?

WENDIE: She is a portal.

PAIGE: How is she a portal?

WENDIE: Many beings are attracted to her light and she's holding on to them until she can get them to the right place, so they are with her.

PAIGE: How can she tell them to go to the right place? How can she work with them? Does she know now already, or can you give her any advice?

WENDIE: All in due time. We will reveal it to her when she is ready.

PAIGE: Could you tell her what needs to be healed on her body?

WENDIE: There's tense energy in her hip.

PAIGE: Why is there tense energy in her hip?

WENDIE: She's sad. She's sad. She feels sadness.

PAIGE: Is there a way we could take that sadness away and make her happy?

WENDIE: She is transmuting for the collective. She wants to be done transmuting.

PAIGE: What do you mean by transmuting for the collective? I don't understand that.

WENDIE: She's processing energies. She's agreed to this before she came here.

PAIGE: Is that what makes her sad?

WENDIE: She's not yet learned that she does not have to feel every drop of sadness that comes through her.

PAIGE: How can we get her from not feeling every sadness that goes through her? What can we do about that?

WENDIE: She should shield and understand from a higher perspective.

PAIGE: How can she shield it?

WENDIE: Meditation. She should surround herself in a white light.

PAIGE: Are you healing her hip?

WENDIE: Yes. There are many parts of her that are coming together again.

PAIGE: What other parts are coming together?

WENDIE: When she was young, she was hurt.

PAIGE: How was she hurt?

WENDIE: Somebody hurt her.

PAIGE: Could you let me know when you're done with that part? That hip?

WENDIE: Yes, we are done.

PAIGE: Are there any other parts you need to work on her body?

WENDIE: Her neck.

PAIGE: What's wrong with her neck?

WENDIE: She has a chakra out of alignment. It faces the wrong direction.

PAIGE: How did it get out of alignment?

WENDIE: Stress. She lost hope. She gave up. Sometimes she feels power and she goes to the dark. But her heart knows. She pulls herself back. She does not like feeling not in power, not in control. She's afraid but we are teaching her to live fearlessly now. She says she's already been through the worst so what's to fear, and that is exactly the attitude we need her to have.

PAIGE: Why did you bring her to me today?

WENDIE: You two are sisters.

PAIGE: We are?

WENDIE: You are soul sisters. You are from the same tribe.

PAIGE: What tribe is that?

WENDIE: Pleiades. She knows.

PAIGE: She wasn't sure.

WENDIE: In her heart she knows. She needs to be more sure of herself. Trust herself.

PAIGE: Have we had many lifetimes together?

WENDIE: A few.

PAIGE: I saw something like a star in the sky yesterday. Could you tell me what that was?

WENDIE: It is what you think it was.

PAIGE: Can you say it out loud?

WENDIE: It was a light ship. They're here. They are all over. This is a big time for humanity.

PAIGE: Did they see that I saw them?

WENDIE: Yes. They let you see them.

PAIGE: Are they the ones I saw last week also?

WENDIE: Yes.

PAIGE: Are they gonna make contact with me?

WENDIE: They already have.

PAIGE: They have? When?

WENDIE: When you're sleeping.

PAIGE: I don't remember anything.

WENDIE: (whispers) You will remember when you are ready, dear.

PAIGE: Thank you. Are you done with Wendie's neck?

WENDIE: Yes.

PAIGE: Is there any other part of her body you need to work on?

WENDIE: No.

PAIGE: How's her back?

WENDIE: We will deal with that part later.

PAIGE: Why later?

WENDIE: There is something there. She has an attachment. She has many cords.

PAIGE: Can we forgive and cut the cords today?

WENDIE: Yes.

PAIGE: Can you do that right now?

WENDIE: Yes.

PAIGE: Can you do it for all the lifetimes?

WENDIE: Yes. Saint Germain.

PAIGE: Is Saint Germain helping you with the cords?

WENDIE: Yes.

PAIGE: Let me know when you're done cutting the cords.

WENDIE: It is done.

PAIGE: That attachment, can we deal with it today?

WENDIE: Yes.

PAIGE: Can we have Michael here help with the attachment?

WENDIE: He is here.

PAIGE: Thank you. Archangel Michael, would you help us?

WENDIE: Gabriel is here.

PAIGE: Gabriel, please help us. What is this attachment? Is it a person? A soul?

GABRIEL: It is an entity.

PAIGE: How long has he been with her?

GABRIEL: Lifetimes.

PAIGE: Why is he with her?

GABRIEL: So, she has power. She called upon somebody, and he answered.

PAIGE: But we need to get rid of him now?

GABRIEL: Yes, we do. She no longer needs that energy. It is too dark.

PAIGE: It's too dark?

GABRIEL: It is too dense for her. She can really see that.

PAIGE: We're asking for the archangels. Michael and Gabriel, please take this entity to the light and release it from her back. *(pause)* Is it gone or is there anything else we need to do?

GABRIEL: It is being done.

PAIGE: And we ask that Archangel Gabriel heals that part and seals the area where that entity was. Can he do that for us?

GABRIEL: Yes.

PAIGE: The healing is being done?

GABRIEL: Yes. We're filling her with love light now.

PAIGE: Thank you. Thank you very much. Wendie says there's a star put on by her father on her third eye. She'd like to know if it's still there.

GABRIEL: It is.

PAIGE: What is that star doing?

GABRIEL: He's protecting her. He's guiding her.

PAIGE: That's good. She'd like to know if she and her father have had any lifetimes together.

GABRIEL: They have.

PAIGE: Could you tell me about them?

GABRIEL: He was her father before. He would not let her marry who she wanted.

PAIGE: Why wouldn't he let her marry who she wanted?

GABRIEL: He did not approve. She was very angry with him.

PAIGE: Is there a soul contract we need to complete on this, of this time?

GABRIEL: No.

PAIGE: So why is he her father in this lifetime also?

GABRIEL: He was guiding her. He had much to teach her and inspire her to counterbalance that which she was learning elsewhere that was not full truth. He showed her that there are many, many paths to enlightenment. There's not just one path.

PAIGE: There are many paths?

GABRIEL: Yes.

PAIGE: Wendie would like to know if she's had other lives with her children that you'd like to tell her.

GABRIEL: Yes.

PAIGE: Could you tell me about some of them?

GABRIEL: That will be for another time.

PAIGE: Oh. Okay. Was her soul started in the Pleiades?

GABRIEL: She is Pleiadean.

PAIGE: Could you tell her about her life there or her lives there?

GABRIEL: That is where she received the knowledge she needed to better help her in this life.

PAIGE: What does Wendie enjoy doing in the in-between lives?

GABRIEL: She is in her star. She is a guide to many.

PAIGE: What is Wendie's soul mission here?

GABRIEL: Children.

PAIGE: Children?

GABRIEL: She loves children, and the children love her, and she helps them find their light.

PAIGE: Where is the child she left behind?

GABRIEL: In the soul star. Her children come back. They always come back to her.

PAIGE: Did that child come back as one of her children now?

GABRIEL: No.

PAIGE: So that child is not incarnated on Earth right now?

GABRIEL: Not at this point. She very much wanted a do-over but that is not for this life.

PAIGE: Wendie would like to know if she is a walk in[15]?

GABRIEL: She is.

PAIGE: Is that what happened to her that day that she couldn't remember who she was? Is that when she walked in?

GABRIEL: No. It was before that.

PAIGE: When did she come into this body?

GABRIEL: There was an accident.

PAIGE: There was an accident? When?

GABRIEL: She gave up and she needed to go.

PAIGE: How old was she when that accident happened?

GABRIEL: Twenty.

PAIGE: Uh huh. What happened to that soul that left the body?

GABRIEL: She has moved on.

PAIGE: Why did her skull seem like it separated?

GABRIEL: Her body's changing. Her DNA is upgrading. Her cells are arranging themselves in a way that better suits her needs.

PAIGE: She said years ago she came out of the top of her head. Can you tell me about that?

GABRIEL: That was a crystalline body.

PAIGE: That's what she thought. Was she being activated then?

GABRIEL: She was, indeed.

PAIGE: What was on the head that looked like a small bowl?

GABRIEL: That is her energy center.

PAIGE: Should we worry about her skull looking like it's separated?

GABRIEL: No, she's fine. She worries much. She's fine.

PAIGE: She'd like to know; that bowl on her head, why did that happen? Will that always be purple, or does it charge?

GABRIEL: That is her crystalline color. That is her crystalline body. It is more of a lightish-pinkish purple.

PAIGE: How come at the same time her back was hurt? What happened?

GABRIEL: She fell as a child.

PAIGE: She fell as a child?

GABRIEL: Yes.

PAIGE: Okay. Because I think she thought her back started hurting when she came out of the top of her head.

GABRIEL: She fell as a child, but she did not tell anyone how much she was hurting. She did not want to be in trouble.

PAIGE: Why are the muscles in Wendie's body different on each side?

GABRIEL: She needs to balance her energies.

PAIGE: How does she balance her energies?

GABRIEL: Meditation again. She does not want to have to sit still for long. She has a hard, difficult time with that.

PAIGE: She says the right side is weaker.

GABRIEL: It is.

PAIGE: Why's it weaker?

GABRIEL: Unbalanced energy flow.

PAIGE: That time that she lost her memory, and she didn't remember that it was her house, what happened there? Why did she lose her memory?

GABRIEL: We were working with her. She was suicidal. She wanted to go. She did not want to be here any longer.

PAIGE: So why did she lose her memory?

GABRIEL: We were working with her. We were clearing her.

PAIGE: Is there anything else you can tell me about that?

GABRIEL: She did not know the beauty that she is.

PAIGE: How did you get her to figure that out?

GABRIEL: We had to show her her light. That is why we helped her. With her crystalline body she then saw herself as we see her.

PAIGE: She says she wants to know about the twin souls. How do they fractalize?

GABRIEL: One soul comes through. One emerges with the fetus.

PAIGE: Are her twins twin souls?

GABRIEL: They are. They are of the same soul. They have fractalized into two beautiful, beautiful beings.

PAIGE: Why did they choose Wendie?

GABRIEL: Because she is a wonderful mother and she's loving. She loves them with all of her soul—and she will protect them fiercely.

PAIGE: What is Wendie's Higher Self's name?

GABRIEL: It starts with an "A."

PAIGE: Can you tell me the whole thing?

GABRIEL: No.

PAIGE: Why not?

GABRIEL: There is not a word for it in this language.

PAIGE: Who is Kyra? Why does that name come up?

GABRIEL: That is the name she gave the child she let go.

PAIGE: Oh.

GABRIEL: She does not always remember that.

PAIGE: She'd like to know what other lives she's had on Earth.

GABRIEL: There's been so many.

PAIGE: Can you tell me any details of any of the others?

GABRIEL: Right now, only the one from the farm.

PAIGE: What time period was that one from the farm?

GABRIEL: 1800s. 1886.

PAIGE: She'd like to know what happened to Rick after he left the hospital. How did he die?

GABRIEL: He had a stroke. That's why he couldn't remember anything.

PAIGE: How did he walk away from there?

GABRIEL: They gave him something to help with his pain and he was able to walk that far. He was trying to get to her.

PAIGE: He was trying to get to her?

GABRIEL: Yes. She was his safety.

PAIGE: Uh huh. So, he was walking on his own?

GABRIEL: Struggling, but yes. Once the medicine wore off, he couldn't go any further.

PAIGE: Why did things happen this way?

GABRIEL: To wake her up.

PAIGE: How did it wake her up?

GABRIEL: We do not like seeing her hurting. She lost so much but it had to fall away so we could get in touch with her deepest, deepest parts.

PAIGE: But she felt so guilty and depressed afterwards. How can we take more of that guilt away?

GABRIEL: She did not let her children down.

PAIGE: I know she didn't let them down but how can we take that guilt away from her?

GABRIEL: She needs to understand this was going to happen whether she was there or not.

PAIGE: Could you tell me where he is now? Where is Rick[16]?

GABRIEL: He has crossed over.

PAIGE: That's good.

GABRIEL: He is happy and well.

PAIGE: Are there any messages he'd like to tell Wendie or his children?

GABRIEL: Thank you. Thank you for everything you did for him. That it's not her fault although she blames herself.

PAIGE: I know. She needs to stop blaming herself. Her grandfather, how is he doing?

GABRIEL: He is busy.

PAIGE: What's he busy doing?

GABRIEL: Taking care of children on another planet. He is guiding them. She will join him in another life again.

PAIGE: Does he have anything to say to Wendie?

GABRIEL: He's so proud of her.

PAIGE: He's so proud of her?

GABRIEL: He loves her so much and the pain of the world is not her fault, and she is not responsible to heal it all on her own.

PAIGE: That's good to tell her because she seems to take on every burden.

GABRIEL: She does.

PAIGE: Why did she choose to see so much darkness in this life?

GABRIEL: For compassion. She wanted to see the light *and* the dark. She wanted to understand and see people in their darkest moments so that she could help them see their light.

PAIGE: Her dog, Hachy—seems like a special dog? Who is it to her? Does she know the dog from other lifetimes?

GABRIEL: He's one of her angels.

PAIGE: How is he an angel to her?

GABRIEL: He feels her.

PAIGE: Does she know him from another lifetime?

GABRIEL: Yes. From in between.

PAIGE: What was the dog in the in-between lives?

GABRIEL: Red.

PAIGE: That's how she sees him. Was he a dog in the in-between lives?

GABRIEL: No.

PAIGE: What was he? What kind of spirit was he before?

GABRIEL: An animal spirit.

PAIGE: Was there a shape to him in the in-between lives?

GABRIEL: He is a wolf. He carries the energy of a wolf. She's close with them, all of nature, but she is a light for others. When he is by her side, he helps her process energies. That's why he sleeps next to her.

PAIGE: He helps her process energies?

GABRIEL: Yes.

PAIGE: Sally. What was their relationships in other lives?

WENDIE: She was my mother. A loving, loving mother. She was also my best friend. We've had many lives together.

PAIGE: What message is there for her?

GABRIEL: You are so loved.

PAIGE: Did they come here together?

WENDIE: We did. We did. We are from the same group. We came here together. We've come to this planet many times together.

PAIGE: She wants to know if each of us have a star that we are connected to.

GABRIEL: You can, but you don't have to. There is a soul star for everyone.

PAIGE: There is a star for everybody?

GABRIEL: Yeah. You can go there and recharge at night.

PAIGE: You can? You can go there and recharge at night?

GABRIEL: Yes.

PAIGE: Is my soul star the same as Wendie's?

GABRIEL: No, you have your own.

PAIGE: Could you tell me Wendie's soul star name?

GABRIEL: Polaris.

PAIGE: Should Wendie train to be a QHHT® practitioner?

GABRIEL: Yes, she should.

PAIGE: Will she be a successful one?

GABRIEL: Yes.

PAIGE: Wendie would like to know what qualified her for this life.

GABRIEL: She has seen many dark things and it does not shake her soul. She is stronger than she thinks.

PAIGE: What experience does she have to call upon now?

GABRIEL: She has been doing this for many, many eons.

PAIGE: What talents does she have that remain untapped?

GABRIEL: She will find it pleasurable to run. She does not like to exercise, but she will find it to be freeing, and she will enjoy the pleasure of it. The wind on her face.

PAIGE: So, you want her to exercise?

GABRIEL: Yoga.

PAIGE: Yoga? Are there any other talents that she needs to cultivate?

GABRIEL: Her energy work. She's a natural. She does it for her children all the time. She needs to do it for herself as well.

PAIGE: Laurie—her friend—could you tell me if she is a Pleadian?

GABRIEL: She is.

PAIGE: Why does she have a block to find out?

GABRIEL: She is afraid to know. And she wants to focus on this life.

PAIGE: But she also wants to know where she came from. She really, badly wants to know where she came from. Has she ever had a past life on Earth before?

GABRIEL: No. No. She's Sirius.

PAIGE: Sirius.

GABRIEL: Sirius planet. There is a planet. She has learned much on that planet. She brings those skills here.

PAIGE: She does?

GABRIEL: She is a healer.

PAIGE: Laurie is a healer?

GABRIEL: Yes.

PAIGE: You said she's also from Sirius? Is that a different planet?

GABRIEL: It is a planet over there, yes. She's from there. She has been there.

PAIGE: So, she's from both planets?

GABRIEL: Yes. She has had lives in many places.

PAIGE: But none on Earth?

GABRIEL: This is her first time on Earth. She is here for the great awakening.

PAIGE: Wendie would like to know: does she have a special stone to work with?

GABRIEL: Amethyst.

PAIGE: How will it help her?

GABRIEL: It resonates with her frequency.

PAIGE: Does she have that stone right now?

GABRIEL: No.

PAIGE: How will she find it? Does she need to find the right one or any amethyst?

GABRIEL: Any amethyst.

PAIGE: How can Wendie handle the darkness and cruelty of other people?

GABRIEL: She needs to remember we are waking up at our own pace and people who are waking up slower are not a threat. There is no one to fear. She should shield, use her shields, and remember her Higher Self. We tell her that all the time.

PAIGE: What should she do about her mother? The darkness and cruelty about her mother?

GABRIEL: Teach her children to shield.

PAIGE: Teach her children to shield?

GABRIEL: Yes.

PAIGE: Is there anything she needs to say to her mother?

GABRIEL: I forgive you.

PAIGE: That's a good one. Is there any way to keep the negativity of her mother away from her?

GABRIEL: We will help her. She should shield. Wendie will shield and her mother will learn.

PAIGE: Mmm.

GABRIEL: Yes. She remembers. Just love.

PAIGE: Wendie would like to know how she can help to heal the water in the lake.

GABRIEL: She will be activating the lake with crystals. She has done this for a while.

PAIGE: When will she find this out?

GABRIEL: Today.

PAIGE: Today? So, can you tell me how she can do that?

GABRIEL: She will be using Reiki.

PAIGE: On the water?

GABRIEL: And on the rains going into the lake.

PAIGE: Mmmhmm.

GABRIEL: And that water will go many, many places and to many, many people and this love she will infuse into the water will go into the people. She will be helping many. She's needed there.

PAIGE: Is that why she's needed there at the lake? For that purpose?

GABRIEL: She lived there before.

PAIGE: She has?

GABRIEL: Yes. She knows the area.

PAIGE: Did she live where the lake resides now?

GABRIEL: Yes.

PAIGE: Where shall she find these crystals to put in the lake?

GABRIEL: Many places.

PAIGE: Are these special crystals?

GABRIEL: People want to help, and they will help her by giving her many crystals to fill the lake with beautiful energy.

PAIGE: People will give her the crystals?

GABRIEL: Yes.

PAIGE: So, she doesn't have to worry about finding these crystals to put in the lake?

GABRIEL: She doesn't need to worry about anything and yet she does.

PAIGE: Well, that's human nature. What's the difference between twin flames and soul mates?

GABRIEL: There is no difference.

PAIGE: There is no difference? Could you explain twin flames to me?

GABRIEL: Those two are created at the same time in perfect balance, the two souls. Not only do they bring out the best in each other, but they also show each other the parts that need to be healed. And as we heal ourselves, we heal the collective and we heal the earth, and she needs that for us. She loves us so much and she wants us to heal.

PAIGE: Who are her soul mates?

GABRIEL: That is for later.

PAIGE: That's for later?

GABRIEL: That is for later.

PAIGE: Did you say I was one of her soul mates?

GABRIEL: You are from her soul group, yes.

PAIGE: Is that the same thing; soul mate, soul group?

GABRIEL: Yes. They are from the soul group. We're a family from the stars.

PAIGE: Mmhmm. Does she have anybody else from her same soul group here?

GABRIEL: There are many. Her soul group is large. There is no need for her to feel alone. There are many with her.

PAIGE: Are her children from her same soul group?

GABRIEL: No.

PAIGE: No?

GABRIEL: Tim.

PAIGE: Tim? Oh, Tim is.

GABRIEL: Lily.

PAIGE: Lily?

GABRIEL: Lily's from Sirius.

PAIGE: Lily's from Sirius?

GABRIEL: Yes. She's a smaller being. They are shorter. They are blue. I see blue. She's beautiful. She's beautiful.

PAIGE: Is she the one that's the granddaughter?

GABRIEL: Lily is Wendie's granddaughter.

PAIGE: Oh. Have Eric and Wendie had other lives together?

GABRIEL: Yes.

PAIGE: Where?

GABRIEL: Egypt.

PAIGE: Did they have a family there?

GABRIEL: I see a bird. A man with a bird head.

PAIGE: Yes, Thoth?

GABRIEL: Yes.

PAIGE: Why do you see him?

GABRIEL: He's pointing at Eric.

PAIGE: Why's he pointing at him?

GABRIEL: He's his guide.

PAIGE: He is? He's his guide right now?

GABRIEL: He is.

PAIGE: Can you tell me anything else about that?

GABRIEL: He was a slave.

PAIGE: Eric was a slave in that life?

GABRIEL: Yes.

PAIGE: Were you a slave also?

GABRIEL: No.

PAIGE: What color was your skin?

GABRIEL: Brown, light brown. We could not be together.

PAIGE: Why not?

GABRIEL: It was not allowed.

PAIGE: Did you have children?

GABRIEL: A son. They took him.

PAIGE: Who took your son?

GABRIEL: This man.

PAIGE: Why'd he take your child?

GABRIEL: He was angry.

PAIGE: Why?

GABRIEL: I wasn't supposed to have a child.

PAIGE: Mmhmmm.

GABRIEL: It was forbidden.

PAIGE: Why?

GABRIEL: I was to stay beautiful and pure. I'm covered in gold.

PAIGE: You're covered in gold?

GABRIEL: Gold powder. They took my son away.

PAIGE: What happened to your son when he was taken away?

GABRIEL: They made him someone special.

PAIGE: Who did he become?

GABRIEL: I don't know. The word "pharaoh" keeps coming to mind.

PAIGE: Is there anything else you'd like to tell me about that lifetime?

GABRIEL: No.

PAIGE: Okay. She'd like to know about her business venture. What can she do to help it go smoothly?

GABRIEL: Be yourself and keep sending love to everyone. Her love is very powerful. She sends it and they feel it and they like that and that is why they like her, and they need her. Again, she helps them see their own light. *(long pause)*

PAIGE: Are Eric's uncles with him?

GABRIEL: Yes.

PAIGE: Could you tell me who Eric's other guides are besides Thoth?

GABRIEL: Michael.

PAIGE: Archangel Michael?

GABRIEL: Yes.

PAIGE: She'd like to surround her grandchildren with the white light of protection. Is she able to do that?

GABRIEL: Yes.

PAIGE: She does that already?

GABRIEL: Yes, she visits them when she sleeps.

PAIGE: Jack.

GABRIEL: Yes, Jack.

PAIGE: Can you tell me anything about Jack?

GABRIEL: He feels everything.

PAIGE: Is it Mary that uses her two fingers as a wand?

GABRIEL: Yes, it is.

PAIGE: Can you tell me more about her?

GABRIEL: There is no veil between her and the spirit world. She is here to balance things out.

PAIGE: What planet does Mary come from?

GABRIEL: She is Fae. She is fairy energy. She has wings. They are yellow. She is Fae. She is an Earth angel.

PAIGE: Why does she *(Wendie)* feel like, in her relationships, they don't really love her? They are misdrawn to her divinity?

GABRIEL: Because she cannot connect to a level that is satisfying to her. She waits for somebody to come and connect with her before she does things. But we keep telling her, "Do it."

PAIGE: Do what?

GABRIEL: All the things she wants to do. Do not wait. Do them, and the right people will come to her.

PAIGE: Are the right people coming to her now?

GABRIEL: She is finding her tribe.

PAIGE: Sounds like it. *(pause)* Was her walk in a contract before Wendie's body was born? Did she know that that was gonna happen?

GABRIEL: She knew, it was a smooth transition.

PAIGE: Was it a contract to happen before the body of Wendie was born?

GABRIEL: Yes.

PAIGE: Who was the lightish-pinkish-purple orb in her backyard?

GABRIEL: It was her great-granny.

PAIGE: What was she trying to tell her?

GABRIEL: She was watching over her.

PAIGE: She was watching over her?

GABRIEL: Yes.

PAIGE: Could you tell why my dog's skin is breaking out?

GABRIEL: It is her food.

PAIGE: Which food is it?

GABRIEL: She needs more pure food. No corn.

PAIGE: So, it is in the dog food? The bags that we buy?

GABRIEL: No corn. No corn. Organic Chicken.

PAIGE: Organic chicken.

GABRIEL: Give her organic chicken.

PAIGE: Could I ask that Archangel Ariel come back and finish healing Sophie's ears?

ARIEL: Yes, we can do that now.

PAIGE: Yes, please do that now.

ARIEL: The energy in the food is keeping her vibrations low. The corn, the corn.

PAIGE: The corn?

ARIEL: The corn is bad.

PAIGE: I didn't realize there was corn in her dog food, thank you. Before we count out...

ARIEL: No wheat.

PAIGE: No wheat?

ARIEL: No wheat. Rice, give her rice.

PAIGE: Give her rice?

ARIEL: Give her rice. No corn.

PAIGE: I know the subconscious could have brought forth many different lifetimes for Wendie to see today. Why did you bring forth that one lifetime?

WENDIE: So she could heal with her daughter.

PAIGE: Why did you pick that lifetime? What does it have to do with this lifetime now?

WENDIE: She needs to know that it's not her fault.

PAIGE: That it's not her fault? Okay, before I count Wendie out, is there anything you'd like to tell her?

WENDIE: She's so loved.

PAIGE: She's so loved?

WENDIE: We are always with her.

PAIGE: You're always with her. Is there anything else?

WENDIE: Meditate.

PAIGE: Meditate?

WENDIE: And build those fires.

PAIGE: Build those fires.

WENDIE: She says she will not wait for a man to build those fires anymore. We want her to be independent but at the same time be able to accept love.

PAIGE: Is there anything else you'd like to tell me?

WENDIE: Meditate.

PAIGE: I'm having a hard time.

WENDIE: Carve out your niche and do not let anything else get in the way. That is the utmost importance. While you are asleep, we will help you. But meditate.

PAIGE: The grounding mats that I bought; will they help me meditate?

WENDIE: Yes.

PAIGE: Okay. I wasn't sure.

WENDIE: Lay on your back in your backyard on the ground and let the earth help heal your body and breathe in the stars.

PAIGE: Breathe in the stars?

WENDIE: Yes

Wendie – Part II

This chapter is about the many sessions that Wendie and I have done together. One day Wendie came to my house, and she felt she had an attachment in her foot. I asked why she keeps getting attachments on her foot. I am told it is because of a previous foot injury. I asked to close the portal on her foot.

PAIGE: Archangel Michael, scan for entity attachment.

ARCHANGEL MICHAEL: Her ankle.

PAIGE: What is in it?

MICHAEL: A gray alien.

PAIGE: Please put the symbol on the gray. Gray in the ankle, I want you to come up up up. Greetings, love, honor, and respect you. May I ask questions?

GRAY: Yes.

PAIGE: What made her open that you were able to attach to her?

GRAY: She is our path.

PAIGE: Path for what?

GRAY: For where we are trying to go.

PAIGE: What was your job in the past?

GRAY: Watcher.

PAIGE: What did you do in the past?

GRAY: I developed machinery that helped me watch.

PAIGE: What are you watching?

GRAY: Humans.

PAIGE: Are you doing anything negative to them or positive?

GRAY: I mean no harm.

PAIGE: I'm just trying to figure out what your mission is.

GRAY: To learn.

PAIGE: Is there an entity above you that controls you?

GRAY: No.

PAIGE: Can I help you spread your love light now and have you positively polarize?

GRAY: My name is Albonia. I'm from a ship. It is just me.

PAIGE: Is there any other information you can give us?

GRAY: I do not want to lose everything that I have learned.

PAIGE: You will be able to keep all of your memories. You will be able to positively ascend. I will have Archangel Azrael lead you safely where you need to go, and I want to follow and see also.

GRAY: I don't want to leave my ship, but I will.

PAIGE: Is there anyone else on the ship?

GRAY: It is just me on the ship. It is my own device I use for tapping in and looking at people. Watching them and learning. I can see them.

PAIGE: So, did you see Wendie and know that she was a way for you to positively ascend?

GRAY: I've watched her for years.

PAIGE: What did you learn about Wendie?

GRAY: She likes to push things to the last minute and then she stresses.

PAIGE: Any advice for her?

GRAY: Don't push things to the last minute.

PAIGE: Can I help you spread your love light right now and help you to ascend?

GRAY: I am empty. I am lonely.

PAIGE: Look within and spread that love light. Every cell. Every piece of your body. I'm helping you. I'm sending you my love now.

GRAY: I am filled with love light. I am a very tall man. I look human but very tall.

PAIGE: What happened that you turned into a gray?

GRAY: I don't know. We need to dissolve the ship so that it cannot be misused by another.

PAIGE: Who can I call on to dissolve the ship?

GRAY: Archangel Zadkiel.

PAIGE: Archangel Zadkiel could you please dissolve the ship for us?

ZADKIEL: It's on fire now.

PAIGE: Thank you. Archangel Azrael, please come in and lead this man where he needs to go. I'm going to follow you. Go ahead and speed up time to where you need to go.

GRAY: It's beautiful.

PAIGE: Where is it?

GRAY: Saturn.

PAIGE: Why did you go to Saturn?

GRAY: There is a hole at the top where you can go inside and there are bases.

PAIGE: What are you going to be doing in Saturn?

GRAY: Recovering and learning to sustain my own energy. I got to remember who I am.

PAIGE: Good. Are your memories coming back now?

GRAY: No, the feeling of who I was, are back.

PAIGE: Who were you before?

GRAY: Albonia is my name.

PAIGE: What kind of body do you have now?

GRAY: Human. but I am nine feet tall. Very long arms.

PAIGE: What color is your skin?

GRAY: Old man.

PAIGE: What kind of race are you?

GRAY: I don't know. I see no one else like me here.

PAIGE: Why are you still an old man? Wouldn't you go back to when you were young?

GRAY: This is where I was the happiest.

PAIGE: What planet did you come from?

GRAY: Sirius.

PAIGE: What do you look like?

GRAY: Gray hair. Human-like face but very long.

PAIGE: Do you remember how you became a gray?

GRAY: We tricked ourselves. They allowed it.

PAIGE: How did this happen?

GRAY: While Shiva slept. He is back now.

PAIGE: Who's back?

GRAY: Shiva.

PAIGE: Is Shiva a God?

GRAY: Shiva is a God. Shiva is also Michael.

PAIGE: I didn't know Shiva was Archangel Michael.

GRAY: Indeed.

PAIGE: I'm trying to understand how this could have happened. I'm trying to understand how you could trick yourself into becoming grays.

GRAY: We thought we were invisible. And we were arrogant. We were naïve and foolish.

PAIGE: What planet were you on at that time?

GRAY: Earth. Many times, the same situation happens over and over until we get it right. This time we will get it right. Shiva woke up.

PAIGE: Can you explain more? Was this the time of Atlantis?

GRAY: Yes. Time of Atlantis and many changes since then.

PAIGE: Can you explain this a little bit more?

GRAY: Humanity gets to the brink and then they do not have the fortitude to stand on their feet and own it. So, they lay down in defeat and may start over. And society builds up again and we go through the same thing again and again until we get it right and we will get it right. Not just humanity. We are all one brotherhood.

PAIGE: Why does Wendie have asthma?

WENDIE: She drowned in a past life.

PAIGE: Can I ask for Archangel Raphael to heal her so that she does not have asthma anymore?

WENDIE: She needs to stop putting the toxins into her lungs. That will help her with this life. There is trauma from a past life.

PAIGE: Can we heal the trauma in the body from that past life?

WENDIE: Yes. She needs to see that she died to help her brother survive.

PAIGE: Should we take her back to that past life?

WENDIE: Yes.

PAIGE: Okay, go back to that past life. Be there now. What is happening?

WENDIE: We are fishing in the lake. Just us.

PAIGE: What happens next?

WENDIE: He is about five or six and I am about ten. We are playing on the boat, and he fell in. He was trying to catch the frog, and he got caught in the tule reeds. We both drowned.

PAIGE: Were you trying to save him?

WENDIE: Yes.

PAIGE: Now take your last breath and go to the other side. What happens when you go to the other side? Who do you meet? What do you do? Where do you go?

WENDIE: She was my friend Sally, and she still loves frogs. She needs to come with me.

PAIGE: Do you know Sally in this life?

WENDIE: Yes.

PAIGE: What do you mean she needs to come with you?

WENDIE: She needs to go to the light.

PAIGE: She did not go to light then?

WENDIE: No. She stayed.

PAIGE: For how long?

WENDIE: Part of her is still there.

PAIGE: Can you go back and get her?

WENDIE: She is with me now.

PAIGE: She is?

WENDIE: Yes. That little boy. My little brother. I love him so much. You're going to the stars. That's where we came from. We came here together and she has her frog. Ha ha ha ha. We are home. Yes.

PAIGE: Can you heal Wendie's body from that trauma from that past life now?

WENDIE: Yes. She stayed there to help her friend and her brother. Thank you.

PAIGE: Are there any other aspects of her past lives that need to come back and be healed?

WENDIE: Button factory.

PAIGE: What happened in the button factory?

WENDIE: She was working in the button factory and there was a man there. He was making advances towards her; she did not want that. He pushed her off a scaffolding.

PAIGE: Did he kill her?

WENDIE: Yes. She did not leave there.

***

THE NEXT SESSION, I TAKE Wendie to the past life in the button factory. She was complaining about her back hurting before the session.

WENDIE: She's still lying on her back. Her dragon is helping her up. Archangel Raphael is taking her for healing. I want you to talk to the man that pushed me.

PAIGE: I would like to talk to the man that pushed Wendie.

MAN: Yes.

PAIGE: Why did you push this woman over?

MAN: She was nothing.

PAIGE: She was nothing? She was a beautiful soul. Why would you do such a thing?

MAN: She had an attitude.

PAIGE: But you just killed a life. Don't you have any remorse for that?

MAN: She was nothing.

PAIGE: She was not nothing. She was a beautiful soul that you hurt and destroyed.

MAN: She rejected me.

PAIGE: So, you're going to do that to every woman who rejects you?

MAN: No. Just her.

PAIGE: How would you feel if someone did that to you?

MAN: It's the way of life.

PAIGE: No, it's not. You have to treat humanity nicely. I want to take you to the last day of your life. Go to the last day of your life. Be there now. Tell me what is happening on the last day of your life?

MAN: I'm alone laying on the ground and dying. Did anybody come? Nope.

PAIGE: Because you treated everyone badly, so you died alone. Now take your last breath and go to the other side. Who meets you there?

MAN: My mother.

PAIGE: What is she telling you?

MAN: She's sorry that my father hurt me.

PAIGE: Is that why you turned out the way you did?

MAN: She did not protect me.

PAIGE: Maybe she did the best that she knew how to do.

MAN: He hurt her too.

PAIGE: She did the best she knew. She tried her best.

MAN: (crying) I love my mother.

PAIGE: I want you to embrace that love and hug her.

MAN: She says that I shouldn't have hurt that woman in the factory. I'm sorry. *(continues crying)*

PAIGE: Tell Wendie that.

MAN: I'm so sorry. I'm so sorry.

PAIGE: Wendie, what do you have to say to this man? Do you forgive him?

WENDIE: I forgive you. Don't let it happen again.

PAIGE: I send this man off with love and light.

MAN: Thank you.

AFTER THE SESSION WENDIE TELLS me that the man turned into a little boy while talking to the mom. Wendie's back was healed and so was that aspect of her from that lifetime.

***

IN ANOTHER SESSION WITH WENDIE, I was curious about our past lives together.

WENDIE: Wendie and you go way back. She is here to assist; you are siblings.

PAIGE: What lives have we had together?

WENDIE: You were in the village when she ran from the religious leaders. The government was chasing her out of town. They wanted her dead. She was accused of being a witch. She was a healer. She found a village and you were in the village. You fed her and kept her warm. She is recalling those people that helped her in her past lives and is finding them in this life. And doing everything she can to give them the love that they deserve. The village life was cold and muddy, but your home was warm and comfortable. And she is still very grateful for that. You had a little boy then. His name was Joshua. You made a mean stew.

***

I REALIZED THAT WE COULD talk to someone else's Higher Self through Wendie when she is under hypnosis. In this session we take a reptilian off of our friend, Betty. This reptilian was negatively polarized and could be mean. Wendie could see Betty's soul cowering in the corner.

PAIGE: Could I speak to Betty's Higher Self?

BETTY: Yes.

PAIGE: Could we take the reptilian off of you?

BETTY: If you think you can.

PAIGE: Let me speak to the reptilian.

REPTILIAN: Yeah?

PAIGE: Greetings, love, honor, and respect to you. I'm here to help you today. As you know, Earth is ascending and negative beings like you are not going to be allowed to be here. When Earth ascends, you will have to go straight back to Source. I would like you to retain your memories and have you go to the light. Would you accept my help in going to the light?

REPTILIAN: Not quite.

PAIGE: So pretty soon there won't be a tomorrow, and you will be zapped back to Source.

REPTILIAN: Will I get a life?

PAIGE: Yes. You will feel love. You will be free to do whatever you want instead of being this negative being. You will be able to create your light and have your own life.

REPTILIAN: Well, that sounds nice and all but I'm not necessarily a negative being. Seems that the people around me are negative.

PAIGE: Can you tell me more about that?

REPTILIAN: Well, I'm surrounded by idiots.

PAIGE: Who are the idiots?

REPTILIAN: Everyone. They don't even deserve to be here. They have so much energy and power and they don't even know what to do with it. Humans are ridiculous.

PAIGE: Well, I would like to give you that energy and power.

REPTILIAN: I would be way better.

PAIGE: Okay, let's try it out and see how you do. Spread your love light all around you. *(sending love light to the reptilian with my hands.)*

REPTILIAN: This is nice and it doesn't feel lonely. It's hard being the only smart one around.

PAIGE: Archangel Azrael, please take him to the light and make sure he does not get tricked or fooled along the way. I'm going to follow you. Let me know what is happening.

REPTILIAN: We are turning the corner and we are going up on top of the mountain. It's beautiful and there is light. This is where I will heal.

PAIGE: Thank you. May the light of the universe always accompany you.

REPTILIAN: Thank you.

***

IN ANOTHER SESSION WENDIE TELLS me she has a reptilian in the foot.

PAIGE: In the left foot. I want you to come up up up. Greetings, love, honor, and respect you. May I ask questions?

REPTILIAN: Yes.

PAIGE: What kind of entity are you?

REPTILIAN: The kind you normally don't want to mess with.

PAIGE: Are you a reptilian?

REPTILIAN: Indeed. I am here for help.

PAIGE: Why did you attach to Wendie?

REPTILIAN: (very loudly) I am here for help.

PAIGE: Beautiful.

REPTILIAN: She needs to shield. Her light is seen from way too far.

PAIGE: What was your job before you came to Wendie?

REPTILIAN: I control this portal. She closed it. My time is nearing for a new generation.

PAIGE: I'm so glad you want to go. *(rubbing my hands together and sending love light)* I'm going to help you spread your love light. Look within your body and find that light within you. Spread it throughout your whole body. Every cord. Every piece. Every part of your body. Let me know when you have spread that love light.

REPTILIAN: I can see it.

PAIGE: Beautiful. Keep spreading through every piece and part of your body. Go ahead and take all of yourself out of her body.

REPTILIAN: Yes.

PAIGE: Thank you. Do you have a message for Wendie before you go?

REPTILIAN: She needs to shield. She needs to cloak. We can see her light from across the lake.

PAIGE: Thank you for that message. I'm going to have Archangel Azrael take you to where you need to go.

REPTILIAN: She needs to know that there are others waiting. They are willing to come with me.

PAIGE: How many are there?

REPTILIAN: Six.

PAIGE: I want all of you to spread your love light. *(sending love light)* Let me know when you have done that?

REPTILIAN: Looks like we are beaming up. Yes.

PAIGE: Beautiful. Archangel Azrael, please take them where they need to go so that they do not get tricked or fooled along the way. We want to follow you and see where you go. Tell me where you go.

REPTILIAN: Traveling. Turning right and there's a place we follow the spiral down. There's buildings and a place. Trees. This is my new home for now until I learn.

PAIGE: Could you tell me what place you went to?

REPTILIAN: Hawkinine.

PAIGE: Is that a planet?

REPTILIAN: It is a realm. And we are here to learn to sustain ourselves. We cannot take another's energy anymore. We have to learn to sustain our own and this is what we are here to do.

PAIGE: Beautiful. Thank you for taking this next journey.

REPTILIAN: Thank you for helping me find it.

PAIGE: May the light of the universe always accompany you.

REPTILIAN: And you.

PAIGE: Thank you. Archangel Raphael, would you please seal and heal Wendie's foot with your beautiful green light?

RAPHAEL: Done.

PAIGE: Higher Self, is there any more healing on the lake that she can do?

WENDIE: She needs to finish clearing the water of the drownings.

PAIGE: Why did people drown?

WENDIE: Some, it was simply their time, but others weren't ready. They didn't want to go.

PAIGE: What caused them to drown?

WENDIE: Larraina.

PAIGE: Who is Larraina?

WENDIE: She is a dark water spirit. She likes to hold some down. We can speak with her.

PAIGE: I would like to speak to Larraina? Can I speak to Larraina?

LARRAINA: Yes.

PAIGE: Greetings. We love, honor, and respect you. Thank you for talking to us today. I would love to help you ascend and go to the light. Would you allow me to help you do this?

LARRAINA: I don't know if that is possible for me.

PAIGE: Well, would you like to try? As Earth is ascending, negative polarized beings like you will no longer be able to be here. We would love to help you be part of the light.

LARRAINA: I will be a mermaid.

PAIGE: That would be beautiful.

LARRAINA: Would you help me?

PAIGE: Yes. I would love to help you. See that spark of light inside you. Spread that love light to every piece and every part of your body.

LARRAINA: I didn't want to hurt them. I just wanted them to be with me. I'm so lonely down there.

PAIGE: I understand. We have all played our parts and that is of the past and we are all forgiven. It's time for you to come to the light.

LARRAINA: Yes, yes. Thank you. I am here. I am shimmering.

PAIGE: Beautiful. Have you spread your love light?

LARRAINA: Yes.

PAIGE: Where should you go on your next journey?

LARRAINA: I will stay here in the lake and be a helper now. I will lift them up when they fall in. I won't hold them under anymore. I will lift them up and help them breathe. I won't take their breath.

PAIGE: Thank you, Lorraina. May the light of the universe always accompany you.

LARRAINA: Thank you.

***

IN THIS SESSION WITH WENDIE, a tall mantis entity wants to speak to us in our session. Wendie tells me afterwards that she could feel him standing next to her and that he was a positive being.

The mantis looks like a praying mantis insect but they are much bigger than humans.

MANTIS: We are here to help you to make it to the next dimension. We are not here to harm. Although some of us are negatively polarized, the ones that are assisting you today are not. We want you to know the vibration and frequency in your home is conductive with the higher spiritual learning environment and when you have your gathering, we are there. We are there and helping cleanse people that walk through your front door.

PAIGE: Are you talking to me and Wendie personally?

MANTIS: You have a group that you work with. They are here to assist your group. Wendie calls it a tribe. You will be expanding your tribe. And we would like to thank you for your effort and all the things you are doing to help humanity. And we would like to thank you for your consistency.

PAIGE: Could you help me with my seeing and hearing you?

MANTIS: We are beings that live in frequency. When you tap into it, you will be able to hear frequencies. When your ears ring. Your head buzzes. Your eyes vibrate. When you look the other direction, you will feel buzzing in your fingers. You will feel buzzing in your toes. The back of the neck. Feel buzzing in your chest. That is us. We are communicating to you on a frequency level. We are keeping your frequencies clear. We are helping keep the frequencies around you clear. We cannot work miracles. We cannot take care of the frequencies that you choose to be around that are not of the highest vibration. We need you to work on keeping your vibrations as high as possible. When you have problems with that, you can tap into us. We are beings of frequency and vibration. We are here to assist you.

PAIGE: Do you have any advice for me?

MANTIS: Play. Play every day. Laugh, play. That is the frequency of a child. That is the frequency that you create. That is the frequency of love. Do not get stuck in patterns, do not get stuck in routine. Break it up.

I had heard that coffee could be bad for you, so I asked Wendie if I should stop drinking coffee.

WENDIE: Caffeine stimulates the brain in certain spaces, and it leaves other spaces dark with less stimulation. It creates an imbalance. The imbalance is created by those external chemicals. I can see the brain and certain parts are lit up. Certain parts are dark. The caffeine keeps stimulating certain parts of the brain over and over and over stimulates certain thought processes and it leaves others in the dark. For we need more of a consistent natural energy flowing through the brain without focusing on specific parts just to give us energy.

PAIGE: Is caffeine interfering with me seeing and hearing certain frequencies?

WENDIE: Yes. When the frequency of the brain smooths out, those parts of the brain that are dark will light up. The parts of the brain that are too lit up will calm down. You will find a smooth consistency in your energy and frequency of that will then open your third eye. It's all in balance.

PAIGE: Does it prevent me from astral travel?

WENDIE: That imbalance in the brain prevents many.

PAIGE: How long will it take for my brain to get balance?

WENDIE: Three to six weeks. After that, I see smooth beautiful frequencies lighting up.

Sandy

S andy came to me because she was a big fan of Dolores Cannon. Sandy had so many questions and wanted to receive clarity. She was also very kind to allow me to ask a few of my own questions and gave me full permission to allow the Higher Self to give me any information I personally needed to hear. I learned to do this as, sometimes in Dolores Cannon's sessions, the Higher Self of her clients would give her information about herself. This session was right after I was trained in AURA® Hypnosis.

SANDY: I sense urgency to help. I feel female.

PAIGE: What are you wearing?

SANDY: I had to wear what they wear. Very little. I had to help them.

PAIGE: Who did you have to help?

SANDY: I had to help with my creations. I had to help them escape.

PAIGE: What are you wearing?

SANDY: I'm wearing a top that covers my chest—and ends around my hips.

PAIGE: Are you wearing any jewelry or ornaments?

SANDY: No. I had to make it known that I am one of them, not above them.

PAIGE: What color is your skin?

SANDY: It's tan and dark.

PAIGE: Is there anything else you can tell me?

SANDY: It was beautiful.

PAIGE: Why do people need help?

SANDY: The tides are coming. I need to help them. It is the only way to salvage my creations. I help them live to get them in peace. They help each other with food, music, family, and love. There is one that strayed. He needed the most help. He did not feel like he could help. He went away with what I taught him to create his own.

PAIGE: Who is the person that you helped?

SANDY: He did not like that a woman was helping. He felt anger towards me. He felt that he could do better. He was one of us, but he felt he could do more.

PAIGE: What happened to this man?

SANDY: He left. He took others with him. He left with a group. They traveled away to get to the opposite side. He met with someone on a boat, and they traveled.

PAIGE: Move the scene forward, what happened next?

SANDY: *(crying)* He uses his anger with his powers. He forges a hierarchy. He felt he was above everyone there because they thought of him as some god. He was just like us. He felt above them and used this for his advantage. He did horrible things.

PAIGE: What horrible things did he do?

SANDY: He ordered everyone to obey him. He could give them death. He would sit there and paint his face into the skulls. People came to him because they thought he was a god, but he wasn't. He was just like us. I see him by a pyramid. He has paintings on his face. He would order people to do things. Very horrible things. He did not lift a finger. He went into their minds to do this. He made them fight against each other. He made them feel separated. He made them feel like they had to fight for everything that was available because he made them think that there was not enough but there was enough. They fought. They dominated cities and killed. He had his people by him that would help him. He made them believe they were special because they were helping him, and they would be like him one day.

PAIGE: Were you a god yourself?

SANDY: I had to help. I had to come down and help. It was the only way to help them. I don't like that word. I don't like the word "god" because of how bad it is to the ego. There is a connection.

PAIGE: Did that man come from above to help the people in the beginning?

SANDY: No. He was part of the people that were brought to the island. Something happened to him. He was influenced in a bad way. I felt like it was my fault.

PAIGE: Go forward in time where something important is happening.

SANDY: We all decide to come—to come down to put an end to that. We all came to a desert. People were there. All the people were there.

We were there to tell the people to not idolize us. To work together and realize they can help each other. Do not be so separated. There were a lot of people there after the flood. They were so scared. They thought we were gods, but we were just like them.

PAIGE: What happens next?

SANDY: We go to the pyramid. We went in and all sat down. We talked and set a plan because we saw the direction and we had to stop it. I see it's dark but there's light in there. It's dark but we can see them, and we talk. He noticed that we could help them, but he could not do what he did before. We had to do something else. We made a plan that lasted over thousands of years because we understood the karma that had to happen. So, we planned to come back where the water falls. Now we are here.

PAIGE: Are you talking about this time or in the past?

SANDY: We planned to come back at this time because it was there, but it was not strong enough. It needed more light, so we decided to come at certain points, which is now.

PAIGE: Can you explain more how you stopped that man?

SANDY: We could not stop that man. He was influenced by something we noticed in other places, other planets where this was happening again. So, we knew. The man thought he was something greater than he was because he was influenced in a dark way. We knew what would happen again.

PAIGE: What other beings came down to help you?

SANDY: We worked together. We are like friends that assist Earth and other planets like Earth. We hear calls from inside, we come and work together. They were from a time where I was from. They are very interested in Earth because they created it, too. They helped to see everything all the time, even when they are not here. They have many names. They assist but most importantly they are loved.

PAIGE: Let's leave that scene and go to another important time where we will find answers.

SANDY: We are having a discussion away from Earth so they do not hear us. We are in the sky talking about plans to help. We brought ideas but we couldn't agree. This happened for some time until we finally decided to send help inside. We have friends in other galaxies, and we called them to come and help and they were so happy; they helped, and they loved. Some got stuck but we came in to help them out again. We knew this man long ago was the breaking point. He also has a job that he was not aware of, but we helped and came in with other friends from all over. They even came through the sun and through bodies of planets. They wanted to and they also were scared because they could get trapped.

PAIGE: Does the evil man have a name?

SANDY: Tlactecuht.

PAIGE: Is he written about in any history books?

SANDY: He uses anger. He channeled his anger in everything he did. He's hidden but in the open doing this. He was from a time when nothing makes sense to him. That's why he chose this path. To feel something different. He deeply, deep down, knew he was wrong. He was depicted as a being from the forest. His tongue is out. He demanded people create him in art. When he was drawn, he always had his tongue out and his face looked angry.

PAIGE: What time period are you talking about?

SANDY: He came and left because he knew how. He would come into forests in times of vulnerability. Humans were asking for help. He appeared demented and then came back at other times. He popped in and out. So, there is no exact timeline. He always came back to older people to influence them and scare them.

PAIGE: I ask to speak to the Higher Self of Sandy.

SANDY: Yes.

PAIGE: Why did you choose to show her that lifetime?

SANDY: To answer her doubt and show her the root of it all.

PAIGE: What time period is that?

SANDY: In the beginning of her creations. She was a part of it. She was assigned to help evolve beings. She wanted to help directly and that's why she remembers this so vividly.

PAIGE: Was there a name for that time period?

SANDY: There were many names at that time. But yes, mostly Lemuria.

PAIGE: Is he here at this time period?

SANDY: He is here but he notices he cannot interfere. He gave in and assigned himself to help instead of being corrupt. He chose the path of light because he saw the wars he created and now are irreversible. He honored himself to the light to help to reverse what he taught.

PAIGE: What corrupted him back in that time?

SANDY: Jealousy. He saw Sandy as someone that everyone honored. She never, never liked this. She always told them that she was like them, but he hated that she did not use her powers to do things. He wanted more.

PAIGE: Could you heal her back?

SANDY: Yes.

PAIGE: What is the root cause of that discomfort?

SANDY: The root cause is guilt from this lifetime that was shown. She did the best she could. It was not her fault.

PAIGE: Higher Self, scan her body for anything that needs to be healed.

SANDY: She has a tight lasso around the throat. It was put there by entities to shut off her voice.

PAIGE: Could you take that lasso off her throat?

SANDY: Yes, it is done. This was put there by entities and they ran off when they knew we were here. We are healing and putting crystals in her throat. Her voice should change now.

PAIGE: Higher Self, keep scanning her body for anything that needs to be healed.

SANDY: There is a seed in her head. The seed in her head was meant to grow. This is not of ours.

PAIGE: Who put it there?

SANDY: The trickster; the ones that trick and deceive. They meant to plant this in order to gain access to us, visually. She would go crazy when she's hearing things. With her seeing and hearing us she knows she's not crazy. This seed was meant for her to not see and why her eyeball got infected. But we took it out. We turned it to gold, and we planted it back into her head to grow for love.

PAIGE: You keep saying we. Who is "we?"

SANDY: The angels. She knows we are here.

PAIGE: Could you tell me who those tricksters are?

SANDY: They wear business suits in public. They look like you and her, but they are not like you and her. They work with electricity to send these things. They use power to go into people's minds and plant these seeds. They are all going away now. They know what's coming into their life.

PAIGE: Is there a name that you can tell me of these people?

SANDY: They are kind of like what we showed her with that man but there is an influence like the one that was planted into her head. But it did not work, and they are realizing they failed and they are just giving up. They look very wrinkly and green. They have sharp claws.

PAIGE: Are they reptilians?

SANDY: They are part reptilian. What you refer to as Draco.

PAIGE: Can they also be Archons?

SANDY: Yes, they welded AI and influence. They use AI—what you say is Archons. People like you and Sandy are aware these entities will be leaving when Earth ascends.

PAIGE: Archangel Michael, can you scan her body for any Archons?

MICHAEL: Her ears. How did we miss this? One, two. There are two, both sides.

PAIGE: Do they need Phoenix Fire?

MICHAEL: They are listening. They are being shut off. I'm taking it out. It's going to feel like a liquid coming out of her ears. Now we are taking them off. It's a small piece of wire. So small. She is pushing it in when she cleans her ears. Small wire, and it's attached to both sides. Now it's being taken off. It has speakers and receivers on both ends so you can hear on one end and speak on the other side. These are common but they are very hard to find. They are so tiny. Sometimes if we do not look hard, we may miss them.

PAIGE: How come she doesn't have any reptilians on her?

MICHAEL: Because she came in already knowing who she was. So, she came with a barrier before she decided to come. The barrier makes these things harder to get to her. When she is angry or sad or low, they take the opportunity to go in and put the implants into her mind. But she does not have any attachments because they are fearful of what she could do, and she could expose them to her friends.

(The rest of the session was redacted for privacy reasons.)

Sara

This session was done with a QHHT® friend in 2019. Only the life she saw is written down here. As she wants to remain private, I have changed her name to protect her identity. I asked Wendie in a session if it was important to put Sara's session in this book and Wendie said yes. Everyone is capable of having a life like Sara's. This session is really surprising to me. I did not know it was possible. I asked Wendie if this was a past or future life. She said the future and now—because all our lives are actually happening at the same time.

SARA: The first thing that comes to my mind is a sea.

PAIGE: Tell me more. Is there anything else? Do you see land?

SARA: I feel like I'm in the sea.

PAIGE: What else do you see in the sea?

SARA: I can see the sky from the sea. It's like I am floating.

PAIGE: Are you floating in the air?

SARA: I don't know. Maybe.

PAIGE: What color is the sea?

SARA: It's blue. The sky is blue. Everything is blue. There are two suns. It's like the information comes. There're two suns, and it's somewhere else.

PAIGE: What else do you see?

SARA: *(laughs)* You know what I see? *(laughs)* It's a UFO.

PAIGE: Can you tell me the shape of the UFO?

SARA: Oval shape with a dome. Like the classic UFOs but it can land on the sea.

PAIGE: What does it do when it lands on the sea?

SARA: It's taking samples.

PAIGE: What is it taking samples of?

SARA: I think from the sea. They want to see if it is capable of having life in it.

PAIGE: Tell me more. Are you the one taking samples?

SARA: I think so, yeah. It's like a mission there.

PAIGE: What else are you doing there? Can you tell me more?

SARA: We need to know what fits. If we have everything to sustain life.

PAIGE: There's no life on Earth yet?

SARA: It's not Earth, it's somewhere else. It has life but not the kind that we know of.

PAIGE: What kind of life does it have?

SARA: Spirit type of life but not physical.

PAIGE: Is there any life in the sea?

SARA: Yes, but it's not like fish and dolphins. It has spiritual life and spiritual beings but they are not in the body.

PAIGE: Do you perceive yourself to have a body?

SARA: I'm not sure. No. I feel like I am observing all of this. Like all the spiritual life and taking samples.

PAIGE: Are you the one taking samples?

SARA: (laughs) I think I *am* the planet.

PAIGE: Oh, that's very interesting.

SARA: (laughs) That *is* interesting.

PAIGE: That's okay. Can you describe more and tell me more?

SARA: So, there's like beings that bring life on me. We have an agreement.

PAIGE: What is the agreement?

SARA: Oh, oh, they are the Keepers. Like a race, to look after me.

PAIGE: Can you talk to the Keepers?

SARA: They are not there yet. I am trying to see if I am ready to have them.

PAIGE: Is the UFO guy ... one of the Keepers?

SARA: No, no. They are the Seeders.

PAIGE: Oh, that is very interesting.

SARA: Wow, wow. It is like giving birth. To have life on you.

PAIGE: Move forward. When there is life on your planet. You are there now. Tell me what is happening.

SARA: Oh, it becomes more lush. First it was only water and now there is land. It's lovely. There are trees. I can feel the trees.

PAIGE: Can you talk to the trees?

SARA: I think so, if I tried to.

PAIGE: Talk to the trees and tell me what they say.

SARA: Oh, they are wise. They say we are connected. They can hear me.

PAIGE: That is beautiful. What are you telling them?

SARA: I am all about love and I love them and I am so glad they are in my body. So glad.

PAIGE: Are there any more life forms?

SARA: There are humanoids. Humanoids came. I think they are the Keepers.

PAIGE: Are they taking care of your planet?

SARA: I think so, yeah.

PAIGE: How do they take care of your planet?

SARA: Something to do with the energy. They can connect to me. They can connect to the Universe.

PAIGE: Do they talk to you?

SARA: Not in the sense of talking as you know.

PAIGE: What do you feel about them?

SARA: I don't know if they feel. They are like cells in my body. I feel connected and I feel everything that they do. And I love them.

PAIGE: What else are the Keepers doing?

SARA: I don't know if they are that much aware of me.

PAIGE: Are there animals on your planet?

SARA: There are animals.

PAIGE: What kind of animals are there?

SARA: I see birds and sea creatures. Creatures on land and fairies.

PAIGE: Can you describe the fairies?

SARA: They are small.

PAIGE: Do they have wings?

SARA: Yes. But the wings are rainbow colored and not everybody can see them. Some are more connected than others. It's like it is here. It's surprising that life is similar.

PAIGE: Is there anything else you would like to tell me?

SARA: I don't think so.

PAIGE: Now, let's leave that scene and move forward to an important day. A day that you would consider to be important when something is happening. What do you see?

SARA: I am angry.

PAIGE: Why are you angry?

SARA: I don't know. They did something that they should not be doing.

PAIGE: Who was this that did something?

SARA: The Keepers.

PAIGE: What did they do?

SARA: Something to my body.

PAIGE: It will clear up as you speak. What did they do to your body?

SARA: I don't know. They are not taking good care of me.

PAIGE: What are they doing to you to not take good care of you?

SARA: They are like drilling in me. Drilling in me. I can feel it. I don't like that.

PAIGE: What's the purpose of drilling in you?

SARA: Because I have crystals.

PAIGE: Do you want them to take your crystals?

SARA: No.

PAIGE: Why not?

SARA: No, they are beautiful where they are. They have functions.

PAIGE: What is their function on you?

SARA: They are my connection. They connect.

PAIGE: Connect to what? What do the crystals help you connect to?

SARA: Connect to all the beings. Connect to the animals. Connect to my suns.

PAIGE: Who are your suns?

SARA: The two suns.

PAIGE: Oh yeah, you have two suns.

SARA: Because they carry information. I need to know those things and I am so angry.

PAIGE: Move ahead and let me know what happens when they take your crystals.

SARA: There is an eruption. I had to do that.

PAIGE: Why do you have to have the eruption?

SARA: To make them stop.

PAIGE: Do they stop?

SARA: They don't learn.

PAIGE: Do they still keep taking your crystals? What do they do with the crystals?

SARA: I have no idea. They don't know their function.

PAIGE: They take the crystals, but they don't know their function?

SARA: Yeah.

PAIGE: What happens next?

SARA: I have to let them go. They have to go. I am so sorry.

PAIGE: What has to go?

SARA: The Keepers.

PAIGE: How do you get rid of the Keepers?

SARA: I shake.

PAIGE: You shake.

SARA: Yes. It is so easy.

PAIGE: And they leave because you shake?

SARA: They have to pass. They have to pass.

PAIGE: Do all of them pass?

SARA: I think some of them are left. They are the good ones.

PAIGE: That's good. Do they take any more of your crystals?

SARA: No. Now they talk to me.

PAIGE: What do they say?

SARA: Now they are more connected.

PAIGE: They understand you?

SARA: They know their purpose.

PAIGE: What is their purpose?

SARA: They protect me. I love them. I did not know that I could keep the good ones.

PAIGE: That's very good that you could keep the good ones.

SARA: I think they knew. They knew where to go, what to do. I'm so glad that they did not pass.

PAIGE: Is there anything else you would like me to know?

SARA: They will procreate.

PAIGE: Will they procreate on your planet?

SARA: Yeah, and they will fulfill their purpose.

PAIGE: Are you happy now?

SARA: Yeah. That is how it was supposed to be from the beginning, but sometimes these things take time.

PAIGE: Now I would like you to leave that scene and let's move forward to an important day. A day that you would consider to be important when something is happening. We have now moved forward. What is happening?

SARA: I think one of the suns is going to explode.

PAIGE: Tell me more about it.

SARA: It explodes, and it will be the end of this experience.

PAIGE: Now, I would like you to move ahead to what happens next. Let me know what happens next.

SARA: I think it explodes and that system is gone now.

PAIGE: Is there still another sun?

SARA: It's a bit chaotic out there.

PAIGE: What happens to your planet?

SARA: I am seeing where it falls into pieces and there's debris in the space. I think it's gone now and it is okay.

PAIGE: What happens to you?

SARA: It's a nice experience I had.

PAIGE: Where do you go after?

SARA: I don't need to be anywhere. I am everywhere.

PAIGE: Is there anything else you would like to tell me?

SARA: We are so blessed. So blessed. So beautiful.

PAIGE: Now whatever has happened has already happened and you are on the other side of it. From that position, you can look back at that entire life and have a different perspective. Every life has a lesson and a purpose. As you look back at that life, what did you learn from it?

SARA: I learned vastness. It could be so big. You can have life. You can have it flourish. It can end, but it's all okay. It is always fine.

PAIGE: What do you think was the purpose of that lifetime?

SARA: I wanted to experience being a soul of a planet. Like that consciousness. How it goes, how it relates to everything.

PAIGE: I ask to speak to Sara's Higher Self. Why did you choose to pick this lifetime for Sara to see?

SARA: Because she thinks so little of herself. She has to know that she is much, much more.

PAIGE: She is a very special soul for being that planet.

SARA: It was an experience. She liked that. No one is littler than the other. You are all the same. But she has to know that she has much more in her.

***

IF SARA COULD BE A soul on another planet, this teaches us that there is life and energy in everything. Many people know that the Earth's real name is Gaia and she has a soul and intelligence all of her own. We must take care of our planet, Gaia, and not abuse her.

***

I have had two hypnosis sessions where people went to past lives as trees. In my very first hypnosis session was my husband, he went to a past life as a tree. Since it happened during my first session, I wasn't sure about what questions to ask a tree or how to guide him in expressing fine details about his life as a tree. The other session was more recent, and by then I knew what kinds of questions to ask.

From this session, I found out that it was very beautiful to be a tree. The client told me that she felt the golden-brown bark and a breeze going through her branches. She told me: "I just feel so free. It's like my whole body is free again. My roots are so healthy. They wrap around a huge sphere of light. I just feel so tall. I feel the air going all throughout my body. It feels so great; it's going under my bark and into my cells."

Next I asked her to connect her roots to the other trees, and *what does it feel like to connect to the other trees?* She said, "Love. A love that I have never felt before. They are so green so brown and the other trees send messages."

I also asked her if she in tree form has ever communicated with people and she said, "Yes." Her message to them was that "It is time to stand tall. It's time to move forward." She added that it was very emotional communicating with the people, and that her whole body vibrated.

Finally I asked her Higher Self *why did she choose to show the lifetime of the tree?* Her Higher Self said, "It's important because she grows like a tree. Her roots are strong. She has many purposes in this world."

We have many lessons to learn from trees.

***

Thank you for opening up your heart and mind to read this book. I hope that it has taught you that when we expand our minds, we will see how much more there is to learn.

About the Author

Paige Garcia is certified in Dolores Cannon Quantum Healing Hypnosis Technique® (QHHT®) Level 1, Level 2, Angelic Universal Regression Alchemy® (AURA®), Reiki Angelic Alchemy Healing® (RAAH®), Reiki Level 1, Level 2, and has training in Regression Healing. Through her expertise in hypnosis, her clients usually journey to a past life where she is able to help in clearing away trauma to support their healing process. In these sessions, she communicates with each client's Higher Self and the archangels. Paige has learned that through the Higher Self, you can tap into a higher knowledge unaccessed by most people on Earth.

To contact her, email:
Paigebaresoul@gmail.com

Endnotes

1   All session transcripts are reprinted with permission. Some names have been changed upon request.

2   "Higher consciousness (also called expanded consciousness) is a term that has been used in various ways to label particular states of consciousness or personal development. It may be used to describe a state of liberation from the limitations of self-concept or ego, as well as a state of mystical experience in which the perceived separation between the isolated self and the world or God is transcended.* It may also refer to a state of increased alertness or awakening to a new perspective.** While the concept has ancient roots, practices, and techniques, it has been significantly developed as a central notion in contemporary popular spirituality, including the New Age movement."

* Source: "Higher consciousness," *Wikipedia,* last modified February 14, 2025, https://en.wikipedia.org/wiki/Higher_consciousness

**The source of this statement is credited to: Miller, H. L., ed. (2016), *The SAGE Encyclopedia of Theory in Psychology, Vol. 1,* Thousand Oaks, California: Sage Publications, pp. 409–411.

3   The etheric body is the first or lowest layer in the "human energy field" or aura. It is said to be in immediate contact with the physical body, to sustain it and connect it with "higher" bodies.

4   The auric field is a colored human energy field that encloses the human body or any animal or object. The auric field has size, color, and vibrations.

5   Arcturians are a humanoid extraterrestrial species native to the planet Arcturus. They are highly advanced, very loving and peaceful beings. They are helping to heal this planet and raise the vibrations.

6   The Pleiadians are a collective of multidimensional spirit beings from the Pleiades star system. The group's mission is to assist humanity with the process of spiritual transformation. The Pleiades star cluster—also known as the Seven Sisters or M45—is visible from virtually every part of the globe. It can be seen from as far north as the North Pole, and farther south than the southernmost tip of South America.

7   The Lyrans are from the planet Lyra and are often described as looking like lions with human bodies.

8   According to the Merriam-Webster online dictionary, to transmute is to change or alter in form, appearance, or nature and especially to a higher form.

9   The Twelfth Dimension is Source. It is not possible to envision the Twelfth Dimension. It is God. Many ancient cultures have defined God as "beyond words." The Twelfth Dimension includes and exceeds all infinities.

10   In Reiki practice, ChoKu Rei is the power symbol and can be generally translated as "Placing all the power of the Universe here, now." It also provides instant energy.

11   According to Oxford Languages and Google, alchemizing means to transform the nature or properties of (something) by a seemingly magical process.

12   The Emerald Tablets are believed to have been written by Thoth, the Egyptian God of wisdom, the divine mediator and counselor, the inventor of writing and the ruler of several Atlantean colonies. According to legend, before he left Egypt, he gathered the records of Atlantis and recorded his extensive knowledge and wisdom. He placed all the documents in the Great Pyramid of Giza that he erected on the entrance to the Halls of Amenti. More information is available via: https://www.ancient-symbols.com/symbols-directory/emerald_tablet_of_thoth.html Date accessed: February 14, 2025

13   Light beings accompany us on this planet. Some are called angels; others are called guardians or beings of light. The beings of light are here to work with us to create greatness on Earth and exist on higher vibrational planes.

14   This is saying that she has never had a life on Earth before. The past life that was shown was downloaded into her memory.

15   According to Dolores Cannon, a walk in is when the soul that is inhabiting a body chooses to leave the body and allow another soul to take its place. According to the author, this can occur around a near-death experience.

16   Wendie still loved her ex-husband, Rick, and helped when he needed her. Wendie was supposed to pick Rick up from the hospital after he was discharged, but he disappeared.

Publisher's Note

Thank you for your readership and the opportunity to serve you. If you would like to share this book, here are some ways:

REVIEWS	Write an online book review
GIVING	Gift this book to friends, family, and colleagues
BOOK CLUBS	Read it with a group of colleagues or friends
EVENTS	Invite the author to be a speaker for your organization Email: *info@citrinepublishing.com*
BULK ORDERS	Email: *sales@citrinepublishing.com*
CONTACT	Call +1-828-585-7030 or email: *info@citrinepublishing.com*

We appreciate your book reviews, letters, and shares.

www.ingramcontent.com/pod-product-compliance
Lightning Source LLC
Chambersburg PA
CBHW021611120626
46545CB00001B/180